**Political Science and
School Politics**

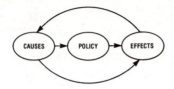

Policy Studies Organization Series

Political Science and School Politics

The Princes and Pundits

Edited by

Samuel K. Gove
University of Illinois

Frederick M. Wirt
University of Illinois

Lexington Books
D.C. Heath and Company
Lexington, Massachusetts
Toronto

Library of Congress Cataloging in Publication Data

Main entry under title:
  Political science and school politics.

  Includes bibliographical references and index.
  1. School management and organization—United States. 2. Education—
United States—Finance. 3. Educational and state—United States. I. Gove,
Samuel Kimball. II. Wirt, Frederick M.
LB2805.P67   379'.151'0973   76-14279
ISBN 0-669-00739-0

Published simultaneously in Canada.

Printed in the United States of America.

International Standard Book Number: 0-669-00739-0

Library of Congress Catalog Card Number: 76-14279

Contents

Preface

Origins

It is appropriate that the National Institute of Education has contributed to the publication of this dialogue between scholars and practitioners of policy. In education there has been a continuing and regular discourse between academicians and the public. The concept of the professional school system, as it emerged out of the conflict within the politician-controlled urban schools of the last century, stemmed in large part from the university. After World War I, specialists in school finance such as Paul Mort at Columbia University inspired the equalization fund concept, which was adopted in every state. In the late 1960s and thereafter, a similar interaction occurred in regard to the equalization policy. Countless concepts that originated in the university have found their way into the practices of professional educators in such areas as curriculum, administration, personnel, and budgeting.

For this book we commissioned a set of papers from scholars and a set of reactions from persons whom we loosely label "practitioners." The latter, in decision-making positions, either presently or in the past, are also familiar with the conceptual and analytical scholarship of their environments. Each provided a set of stimuli and responses focused on a traditional aspect of political science—public administration, mass-elite linkages, federalism, political theory of equality, and Congress. Within each area, five scholars deeply familiar with the particular field carved out some policy implications of current scholarship. Then the practitioners were asked to comment on these ideas from their perspective of the policy world of education.

Schools and Federalism

The contributions are organized only roughly into local, state, and national levels of analysis. The organization is necessarily imprecise because, as is clear throughout, there is intensive, interlevel activity in school policy. While citizen and school professional give much lip service to the value of "local control" of schools, the reality is that such control is becoming increasingly centralized. This is particularly true for the state policy, with its burgeoning mandates and minimums laid on the local school.[1] The federal role in state and local school policy has been a mark of the last dozen years, involving Congress, the Supreme Court, and agencies making policy in such matters as desegregation, financial aid, and student rights. Although in terms of money the federal role is relatively minor (e.g., federal aid to local school costs is only about 7 or 8 percent), its presence in many policy areas is widely noted and reacted to.[2] In the last decade higher education, public and private, has also seen growing participation by state and national policymakers in the amount and quality of that service.[3] Thus while we organize our contributions by level, the interactive process is very much at work. We live in a "family of governments," with the federal principle meaning in reality that intergovernmental cooperation and conflict are the substance of governance in school matters.[4]

Local Focus

Two papers focus clearly on the local processes of school decision making. In exploring the meaning of "innovation" for school administration, Willis Hawley brings together several scholarly interests. What theory suggested about barriers to organizational change has been amply demonstrated in federal efforts to affect school services; and in his distinction between "innovation" and "adaptiveness," Hawley expands our understanding of why that is so. In his comments, Paul Hill sketches the political context of innovation and the professional-official interaction that will make it continue. His expansion of Hawley's concern for adaptiveness suggests the manner in which policy theory can grow once shibboleths are broken.

Harmon Ziegler and his colleagues examine one aspect of elite-mass linkages in interactions between superintendents and interest groups. The work pictures bureaucratic and professional resistance to policy input from outsiders as manipulative actors fending off participatory thrusts from the divergent values of the community. Fred Burke sharply challenges Zeigler's finding, seeing in the world he knows much more highly vulnerable professionals at work amid constantly changing conditions. Moreover, he questions some of the conceptual components of the hypotheses which the other work seems to validate.

State Focus

Donna Shalala and Mary Frase Williams move our focus up to the state level and to financing innovations that recently seemed to be sweeping the states' relation to local school costs. The equalization pressures at work here, the relative utility of the legislature versus the referendum, and the forces that arose to block off further change—all are components of a highly varied set of states in the federal system. In his comments Joel Berke supports this analysis strongly but asks us to note the wider range of political institutions and processes that affect school finance policy. Further, he deals explicitly with the role of the scholar in the policy world, a role he finds wide and impressive in this instance.

National Focus

At the national level, as elsewhere, power and value interact constantly. Our two contributions and responses approach this phenomenon in different ways. Thomas Wolanin shows us the different models used by the scholar and the congressional policymaker when each deals with "facts." Often there is a disjunction, leaving both sides in retreat, shaking their heads about the limitations of the other in the effort to find the "truth." As Wolanin and his commentator Samuel Halperin point out, these two actors are not "wrong-headed"; rather, they start from different assumptions about the nature and the uses of knowledge. The latter clearly are not singular. Halperin adds a helpful corrective in noting that this judgment of Congress deals with only one type of committee; elsewhere things may be different.

We asked Tyll van Geel to focus on the nature of value theory for application to education policy, in particular the work of John Rawls. In a remarkably short time, Rawls's *A Theory of Justice* has had great impact on many scholars of social science.[5] Van Geel draws out the relevance for school policy of this dramatic new departure. This contribution is placed at the conclusion of the symposium, not simply because of its national implications but also because, after a series of writings with certain agreed upon assumptions about who should be schooled and how, it is helpful to look ahead to where we might be going on educational policy. To now, all educational public policy rests on preference in the distribution of resources and values—the provision of empirical and value theories of political science. For the future we may well be greatly stimulated by the work of John Rawls. We are grateful for van Geel's cogent analysis.

We wish to express our appreciation to our contributors of both persuasions for agreeing to undertake their assignments. Very busy men and women themselves, in university or policy arenas (during the course of this work, Professor Shalala was treasurer of New York's "big MAC" board in that city's effort to deal with its financial crisis), they responded well to our proddings about deadlines. We hope their efforts will contribute to the continuing dialogue between the worlds of ideas and actions.

Notes

1. For a review, see Frederick M. Wirt, "State Politics of Education," in *Politics of American States*, 3rd ed., eds. Herbert Jacob and Kenneth Vines (Boston: Little, Brown, 1976).

2. Frederick M. Wirt, "Political Turbulence and Administrative Authority in the Schools," in *The New Urban Politics*, eds. Louis H. Masotti and Robert L. Lineberry (Cambridge, Mass.: Ballinger, 1975), pp. 61-86.

3. Samuel K. Gove and Carol Everly Floyd, "Research on Higher Education Administration and Policy: An Uneven Report," *Public Administration Review* (January/February 1975):111-18.

4. Edith Mosher, "The School Board in the Family of Governments," in *Understanding School Boards*, ed. Peter Cistone (Lexington, Mass.: Lexington Books, 1975), chap. 5.

5. "Justice: A Spectrum of Responses to John Rawls's Theory, "*American Political Science Review* 69 (1975):588-674.

Acknowledgments

The Policy Studies Organization gratefully thanks the National Institute of Education for its aid to the symposium on which this book is based. Thanks are particularly owed to Ray Rist of the NIE.

1 Horses before Carts: Developing Adaptive Schools and the Limits of Innovation

Willis D. Hawley

Introduction

Educators, like other people concerned with bettering themselves and others, are constantly in search of salvation. In recent years the panacea seems to be "change" or, more precisely, innovation. While almost all research on change in public organizations focuses on innovation, the effectiveness of most public organizations, and especially schools, depends less on their willingness to adopt new programs than on their capacity to be adaptive and flexible over time. The argument of this paper is that the capacity of innovation is highly overrated as a source of improvement in education and that the study of innovation yields too little that would be helpful to improving the schools to warrant the attention we give to it.

Innovation and adaptiveness, while related, are different in important ways. Understanding the former does not provide answers on how to achieve the latter. "Innovations" are invariably conceptualized as products or programs that are to be formulated, adopted, implemented, incorporated, and diffused. The "innovativeness" of an organization is defined by its relative speed in achieving one or more of these stages in the process of innovation or by the number of innovations it adopts. Innovations, then, have beginnings and ends. "Adaptiveness" describes the individual or collective behavior of school officials and teachers. "Adaptive people" are creative problem solvers whose behavior is shaped by their diagnosis of problems and resources, both human and technological. Adaptiveness goes beyond reaction to demands, flexibility, or responsiveness to behavior that is aggressively creative, *pro*active, or proformist.[1] It requires continual multidirectional changes in behavior.

To be an adaptive school or teacher is akin to being what M.B. Miles and D.G. Lake call "self-renewing." Such an institution (or person) has "the ability to continuously sense and adapt to its external and internal environment in such a manner as to strengthen itself and ultimately fulfill its goal of providing education for children."[2]

This chapter is, in a sense, a companion to two previous papers on changefulness in public schools. See Willis D. Hawley, "The Possibilities of Nonbureaucratic Organizations," in *Improving the Quality of Urban Management*, eds. Hawley and David Rogers (Beverly Hills, Calif.: Sage Publications, 1974), pp. 371-426; and Willis D. Hawley, "Dealing with Organizational Rigidity in Public Schools: A Theoretical Approach," in *The Policy and the School: New Directions in Education Research*, ed. Frederick M. Wirt (Lexington, Mass.: Lexington Books, D.C. Heath, 1975), pp. 187-210.

This essay reflects a concern that goes beyond the need for adaptive schools, namely, that we have a tendency to define improvements in public policies in terms of new programs, new systems, reorganizations, or more resources. Public policies too often reflect the proverbial triumph of form over substance, of process over product, and of effort over consequence. Social scientists for their part often contribute to all this because we eschew the complex and messy business of studying what happens to the receivers of public policies as a result of their interaction with the services received and those who deliver them. Thus the reforms we advocate often have an otherworldly quality about them that either idealizes the client or neglects the roles government officials actually play. Schools are only one policy arena in which such games are played. While this essay focuses on education, much the same kind of argument could be made about a host of other services including health care, law enforcement, corrections, and welfare programs.

The problem with the emphasis given to educational innovation is not that it is irrelevant. The problem is that the priority given this objective is both out of line with its promise and, more importantly, tends to lead us to put our hopes for improving public policies on doing something new and different rather than on attacking the sources of program or policy failure. In this sense, perhaps less is more.

A number of writers are fond of saying that in education, "the more things change, the more they remain the same." We are also advised by those who study the sources of educational innovation that perhaps the most important determinant of the adoption (but not the implementation) of innovation is "exogenous shocks to the system," that is, demands for change by parents, citizen or professional groups, or other governmental agencies. These two observations combined suggest that innovations are often a way of avoiding more fundamental changes. Innovation, I suggest, is often symbolic politics.[3]

In other words, the adoption and *apparent* implementation of new programs can often create the impression that governments are responding to demands for improved performance. Regardless of the innovators' intent, new programs, reorganizations, and the like suggest that the need for change is recognized and is being acted on. Thus the need to keep the pressure on or to create further incentives for change dissipates. The faster schools innovate, the less momentum external demands for change will gather and the less significant will be the perception that school systems require fundamental change. And this is true for both laymen and professionals.

In the pages that follow, I will suggest why innovations don't "work," why adaptiveness promises to increase the effectiveness of schooling, how one might think about conditions that foster adaptiveness, and the implication of these factors for the structure and administration of schools.

Do Innovations "Work"?

When educators and researchers invest heavily in achieving or explaining the organizational capacity for innovation, even though they know better, they may come to value innovation for its own sake. This predisposition to see innovation as the key to growth in the effectiveness of public schools is manifest in both the scholarly and professional literature. However, those studies that have sought to assess the consequences of planned innovation raise strong evidence that whether a school is likely to adopt innovations may have little to do with its effectiveness in creating a setting in which learning takes place.[4]

There is considerable consensus, aside from the findings of some short-run case studies, that the research on the consequences of major efforts at educational innovation shows little improvement in rates of student progress—at least so far as that progress is measured by cognitive gains.[5] If programs are found to work, the continuity for the child and transferability to other settings are usually weak.

One can, of course, look at a half-empty glass with more sanguine eyes. One very recent study of innovations of the past two decades concludes that they may not have done much good but they have not done any harm.[6] While methodological and conceptual shortcomings in the research on innovation probably result in understating the potential that many of the studied innovations have for increasing the effectiveness of schools,[7] a brief discussion of why the studies have yielded so little evidence that innovations result in substantial improvements in the quality of education should give us some clues as to why adaptiveness should receive more attention.

Innovations "Fail" Because They Are Not Implemented

Students of organizational change agree that it is analytically useful to distinguish between different stages in the innovation process. There are a number of ways the process is described, but the one that appears least complicated and perhaps is most widely utilized is: (1) support or adoption, (2) implementation, and (3) incorporation.

There is also agreement that it is substantially easier to achieve adoption of an innovation than to achieve its implementation and incorporation and that the most important reason for this lies in the inability of administrations and other "adopters" to control teacher behavior.

There is considerable evidence that teachers are in a position to resist or modify innovations and that, despite the appearance of adoption by the school system or the school, the proponents of the innovation would not recognize their plan by observing teacher behavior.[8] The most extensive study of the factors associated with innovation concludes that those programs that are implemented are characterized by "mutual adaptation," that is, the adjustment by teachers of characteristics of an innovation so that it meets their needs or their perception of student needs.[9] As Matthew B. Miles has observed, the installation of an innovation in a system is not a mechanical process but a developmental one in which both the innovation and the accepting system are altered.[10] And John Goodlad, after a study of 100 schools in major metropolitan areas, concluded, "much of the so-called educational reform movement has been blunted at the classroom door."[11]

The research shows, then, that teachers play the crucial role in determining whether innovations are implemented and that innovations can be successful only in adaptive settings.

Innovation Success Is Contextual

To say that an innovation does not work "on the average" or "overall" is to mask a great deal of information. Some innovations work in some settings but not in others, with some children but not others, and with some teachers but not others.[12] The appropriateness of particular innovations to variations in student characteristics, teachers, values and skills, and parental values and behavior seems to account for some variation in their success. Moreover, the significance of these variables depends on the interactions among them. These presumptions pose enormous problems for large-scale evaluative research, problems that have not been adequately resolved by existing studies.

In their extensive study of the factors that might account for variations in the effectiveness of public schools, Averch and his associates concluded that no variant of school facilities, programs, resources, or personnel significantly accounts for variations in student achievements. But they also found that laboratory and small-scale experimental studies—which often come closer than large-scale surveys to resolving the methodological difficulties endemic to educational evaluation—suggest:

... individual methods of presentation appear superior for some tasks and some students but it is still hard to match student characteristics, tasks and type of instruction.
... interaction effects seem to exist among various types of (student and teacher) personality, methods of reward, ability to grasp meaningful material, and so on; but these interactions have not been studied in detail.[13]

Innovations for which cognitive gains are reported tend to be characterized by the emphasis they place on improving the capacity of the teachers to match their skills and programs to the stages of effective and cognitive development at which they find individual students. What all of this adds up to, of course, is that innovations that have significant impact on children depend on adaptive behavior by teachers. I will return to the relationship between adaptiveness and school effectiveness later.

Summary

This brief examination of the research on the consequences of educational innovation leads us to several conclusions:

1. Different approaches to research design and execution would probably result in a better record for innovations. It is not clear, however, that improvements in methodology and conceptualization that will allow definitive conclusions in large-scale evaluations are at hand.
2. No single innovation, unless the innovation involves a high degree of individualized instruction, is likely to make a big difference in the performance of aggregates of children (i.e., classes or schools).
3. The crucial determinant of any given innovation's success is the willingness of teachers to employ it and to do so creatively and selectively in the context of the needs and abilities of their students.

To the extent that innovations are a manifestation of "the symbolic uses of politics," as I suggested earlier may often be the case, one would not expect innovations or innovative schools to be judged effective in terms of significant impact on changes in student performance.

Thus it appears that we are putting the cart before the horse once again, and it is time to invest at least some of the energy that has gone into developing and evaluating innovation into understanding how to create educational environments that encourage teachers and school administrators to be adaptive in responding to educational objectives. Only when we achieve that condition can we expect innovations to provide significant benefits to students.

Adaptiveness and School Effectiveness

Few people will take issue with the notion that schools and teachers should be adaptive. However, the meager resources allocated by either scholars or educational administrators to its attainment suggests that adaptiveness does not have a high priority. Thus there are few hard data that one might employ in assessing the effects of more adaptive school environments on children, and most of what follows rests on theory, observation, and indirect evidence.

For reasons implied above, I take it that the classroom teacher should be our unit of analysis. That is, the relative adaptiveness of schools or school systems depends on the relative adaptiveness of teachers. If such characteristics as what goes on in the community, the superintendent and his staff, the principal's style, student characteristics and norms, organizational arrangements, personal practices, and the like are important to creating adaptive learning situations, it is because these affect the teacher's interactions with students.

While there is substantial disagreement within schools and communities about the specific goals of public education, there appears to be some consensus that the basic concern of formal education should be the learning experience of the student, i.e., the creation of experiences that maximize each student's learning opportunity.[14] There are a myriad of ways that psychologists define learning. A general description that seems to incorporate much of the contemporary research is that of Charles C. Jung, Robert Fox, and Ronald Lippitt:

Learning is primarily a matter of developing the child's total resources for understanding and dealing creatively with his life and the environment within which he lives. Learning deals with analysis as well as memory, with systems as well as isolated units, with behavior as well as thought process. Divergent as well as convergent thinking is appropriate. Emotions are important along with reason. Clarification of values is as much a part of learning as is the discovery of facts.[15]

To define learning is hard enough; to develop an understanding of its dynamics in the context of social environments, including classrooms, is more difficult. A recent survey of the literature on learning theory concludes that among the questions that existing research and theory leaves unanswered are:

1. What are the necessary conditions for learning?
2. What are the roles of practice, of reward and punishment, of stimuli, and of the similarities and differences between them?
3. How do motives influence learning and how are motives themselves learned?
4. What intervening variables can best be used to describe the changes in the organism produced by learning so as to take account of the whole range of possible learning?[16]

It is not surprising, then, that "there is not yet a substantial body of evidence to substantiate a definitive set of desirable teaching behaviors in any one given situation."[17] Moreover, "there is little likelihood that any one given [teaching method] is superior to any other when the overall effects of teaching are appraised."[18]

A recent comprehensive analysis of the research on school effectiveness conducted by the Rand Corporation concludes that, at least as far as cognitive development is concerned, "research has not discovered an educational practice that is consistently effective because no educational practice always 'works' regardless of other aspects of the educational situation."[19]

If any type of educational innovation in recent years can be said to have worked consistently, it is the genre of practices that involve highly individualized instruction. Thus the Rand study cites as representative of other analyses Gordon's conclusions about the relative effectiveness of Title I programs:

The tightly structured programmed approach including frequent and immediate feedback to the pupil, combined with a tutorial relationship, individual pacing, and somewhat individualized programming are positively associated with accelerated pupil achievement.[20]

The emphasis the Rand team placed on structured and sequenced teaching-learning practices is in large part a function of the fact that most individualized instruction programs subjected to evaluation have been of this sort. There is good theoretical reason, backed up by some (weak) empirical evidence that adaptive behavior on the part of teachers in individualized settings would be more effective than less personalized and flexible approaches to programmed learning.[21]

Being adaptive does not mean "doing your thing" or otherwise behaving without constraint. When it is possible to identify certain teaching methods that work for certain children with respect to certain learning objectives, the application of specific routines is obviously appropriate. But the point is that even in these cases teachers must be willing and able to avoid stereotyping children and assuming that if Joanie learns math in one way, the same teaching strategy will be effective in teaching Joanie reading. Moreover, there may well be tradeoffs between what is called for to achieve cognitive development and the way learning should be structured to achieve a capacity for independent thought, a sense of inquiry, or the ability to relate to others.

Even in the most socially homogeneous communities, the range of student capabilities, needs, and motives will vary significantly in any classroom. This fact coupled with the state of our knowledge about how children learn is reason to reemphasize the importance of the teacher to the learning process. David Krathwohl observes in stressing the importance of teachers in integrating cognitive and affective dimensions of learning:

Regardless of how materials are organized to facilitate cognitive learning, it is what the teacher does with these materials that determines whether and what kind of learning occurs.[22]

What does all this mean for the organization of schools? If we can agree that children's learning is the central purpose of schools, we can see from the foregoing discussion that achievement of that purpose rests fundamentally with the quality of the teaching that takes place.

Given the complexity, stress, and uncertainty inherent in the teaching process, one might conclude that the effective teacher (vis-à-vis his or her contributions to a pupil's learning) would be intelligent; possess a flexible, open personality; feel comfortable working with others; be able to see causality in multidimensional terms; be able to tolerate ambiguity; and enjoy spontaneous and intimate student-teacher contact.[23] Such characteristics, as I have implied earlier, could serve as a definition of adaptiveness.

Toward More Adaptive Schools

*Utility of Innovation Research Is Limited in
Understanding Adaptiveness*

At first thought, one might assume that the answers to how adaptiveness could be fostered in schools might be found in the literature on the sources of innovation in public organizations, especially schools. However, there are several reasons why this approach will not take us very far. A brief look at these reasons will not only help distinguish important differences between adaptiveness and innovation but will help to give some context to my later discussion of the factors that influence adaptiveness.

Quality of the Research. Research aimed at explaining why some public organizations are more innovative than others is, taken as a whole, something of a bust. While the number of studies being conducted seems to be growing exponentially, basic questions still go unanswered. Most of the research is plagued with methodological and conceptual problems. Many of the conclusions reached are atheoretical, tautological, or they simply beg the question. No study of which I am aware has attempted to explain how differences in the conceptualizations, measurements, and contexts involved might reconcile the various studies. After an extensive review of the literature on educational change, Joseph B. Giacquinta concluded:

As research designed to test hypotheses derived from theory about organizational change, the quality is poor, and little is contributed to a systematic understanding of organizational change in schools. . . . The literature is basically atheoretical in nature. It contains little work designed to develop and test theories describing the dynamics of the change process or explaining why . . . schools vary in the degree and speed with which they change. Moreover, confidence is not warranted in a number of currently held generalizations about organizational change because the research methods and statistics upon which they are based are inadequate.[24]

And, in any case, those concerned with innovation have not examined the process of incrementalism and adjustment involved in implementation and incorporation except to say that innovations are seldom adopted in their original form.

Some Differences in the Characteristics of Innovation and Adaptiveness. Innovations are usually defined by researchers (in various ways) as major changes rather than incremental or minor adjustments to existing practices. Adaptiveness could result in great instability and inconsistency for both student and teacher if it meant moving from one distinct pattern of behavior to another.

Innovations are usually introduced with the assumption that they should be implemented systemwide or throughout a school. Indeed, some major studies measure the success of an innovation in terms of how widely it is diffused without altering its characteristics.[25] In other words, in contrast with adaptiveness, innovation is seen as providing a right way to do something rather than an alternative to be adapted to situation, teacher, and student.[26]

A key strategy for advocates of innovation is to convince teachers that great improvements will result from the innovation if it is utilized intact. Not only does this lead to excessive aspiration and in turn invariably to frustration and disillusionment, it also focuses attention on process rather than outcome. Adaptiveness requires not only the rejection of the hope for universalistic solutions but also an emphasis on the behavioral consequences of student-teacher interaction.

Most research on innovation is based on products or teaching strategies that are initiated outside the system being studied. This has led to a belief that innovation depends heavily on "exogenous shocks" to the system.[27] Adaptiveness seems independent of such shocks—at least as experienced by the teacher. Indeed, adaptiveness must be internalized by the teacher and may require some isolation from the threat that usually accompanies "shock to the system."

If, as I suggested, innovation sometimes serves symbolic political purposes, understanding the characteristics of schools that have adopted new programs for such reasons will contribute nothing to understanding the conditions that foster adaptiveness.

Innovations usually require *a* decision by the teacher, and they are by definition temporary. There appears to be some agreement among students of innovation that organizational arrangements that encourage the formulation of new plans are different from those necessary to implement them, which may in turn be different from the structures necessary to achieve incorporation of diffusion.[28] But adaptiveness involves both formulation and implementation and requires an awareness that no given innovation can be accepted unequivocably. Moreover, most of the research focuses on the formulation and adoption of innovation but ignores later stages so that the processes by which teachers incorporate and sustain new ideas in their classrooms are not well examined.[29]

Summary. All of this is not to argue that one interested in fostering adaptiveness should ignore the existing research on innovation. But most theorizing about organizational change does not distinguish between innovation and adaptiveness. It is assumed, it seems, that innovative organizations will be adaptive and vice versa. However, while the latter seems logical, the former does not. As I have suggested, an uncritical and deductive use of findings from these studies would be inappropriate and misleading.

Motivating Adaptive Teaching: A Theoretical Model

People will consider changing their behavior when the change promises to move them closer to their goals. But thinking about changing does not lead to change until some calculation of costs and benefits results in a belief that the benefit of movement toward the goals will be sufficient to warrant the costs.

The innovative process is invariably initiated by persons other than the teacher, and the teacher in effect makes a decision whether to be a spectator or a participant who has no commitments beyond the immediate game. Adaptiveness, on the other hand, involves a decision to be in continual search for new ideas and to maintain considerable flexibility in one's behavior. This decision is, of course, demanding and is likely to be made only if one perceives, on a continuing basis, that there are problems that need solving and that solving the problem will result in some net benefit. From this proposition follows the central dilemma involved in securing adaptive schools: It requires the maintenance of the feeling that one's performance should be better than it is.

Most people are utility maximizers; that is, given their resources, they do things that they perceive will move them closer to the attainment of their objectives. Of course, we often have multiple objectives which may compete and sometimes conflict with each other. In considering changes in patterns of behavior or taking on new responsibilities, we ask whether it will be worth it to change or to otherwise extend ourselves; that is, we weigh the benefits of the new behavior against its costs. This benefit/cost analysis in itself has costs, and for this and other reasons our calculations tend to be superficial, imprecise, and conservative. We, in effect, give more weight to costs than to benefits in part because we can see the costs clearly since they are in some measure part of our present. It follows then that we can encourage people to consider behavior changes either by increasing the clarity and magnitude of the benefits or reducing the perceived costs.

To keep matters reasonably clear, I have spoken of change in terms of the kind of considerations one would undertake in dealing with a specific opportunity or demand for change, for example, the decision to adopt and implement an innovation. The decision to be adaptive also involves the assessment of costs and benefits but—at least in the short run—the promised benefits are less specific and calculable. In addition, one is likely to weigh the costs more heavily because the behavior required is long term and much more complicated than the prospect of adopting a single and relatively well-defined innovation. It should surprise no one then that an innovation is easier to attain than a state of adaptiveness.

In any case, a successful organizational strategy for achieving adaptiveness in teacher behavior depends on demonstrating that the benefits exceed the costs and on creating conditions that diminish costs and enhance benefits. Thus an organization must consider three sets of factors for attaining adaptiveness:

1. Factors affecting the perception of a gap between one's performance as a teacher and the objectives one values. This gap depends on both performance and objectives, and the organization might seek to provide information about either or both.

2. Factors affecting costs and the possibilities that these can be minimized. These would include consequences of being adaptive as well as negative sanctions that might be attached to an inability or unwillingness to behave adaptively.
3. Factors affecting benefits, including those that involve material, status, and social rewards as well as those that promote self-esteem or self-actualization.

If an organization can acquire the capacity to affect perceptions in the suggested direction and either reduce costs or increase benefits, or, ideally, reduce costs and increase benefits simultaneously, it will increase the adaptiveness of its members. However, bringing attention to a gap between performance and valued goals without increasing the net benefits one will obtain from adaptiveness will be counterproductive and result in frustration, low morale, defensive behavior, and other unhappy consequences for the children the teacher encounters. In other words, self-awareness and high goals do not necessarily result in better teaching.

Much of the remainder of this chapter examines these three sets of factors in more detail in order to suggest the directions those who seek more adaptive schools might travel. The application of this theoretical framework is confined to the inducement of adaptiveness among teachers.

I will not deal with what causes administrators to favor adaptiveness. I do believe that what I propose about the question of teacher adaptiveness can be employed at any level, though the variables that would be relevant will differ to some extent.

Perceiving a Need for Adaptive Behavior

Adapting one's behavior and staying adaptive depends, as I suggested previously, on the recognition that there is a gap between the goals to which one aspires and one's present capacity to achieve them.

Goal Setting and Adjustment. If goals are to play the role suggested in inducing a predisposition for adaptiveness, they must be explicit, and they must be personalized vis-à-vis students, or at least groups of students. The literature on teacher behavior suggests that while teachers generally aspire to certain idealized objectives such as academic excellence, creativity, and self-esteem for all their students, many find it difficult to sustain a multiplicity of goals, and they tend to narrow their operating objectives to those that appear within reach.

The problem then is to create a setting conducive to teachers' clarifying their goals and being aware of potential outcomes for their students that they otherwise might not have considered or might have ruled out. This atmosphere can be created by structuring and enriching the interactions teachers have with administrators, peers, parents and students, and professional information (journals, coursework, etc.).

Professional Information. I refer here to information about what is going on in other schools or new research that might be relevant to a teacher's general responsibilities and professional interests.[30]

Interaction with Parents and Students. Teachers often shape the goals they have for students without any input from parents or students. It is true, of course, that many parents and children are not very precise or assertive about their hopes, but the capacity to articulate goals can be encouraged, and over time parents and students will learn how to express their aspirations.

Parental and student goal discussions not only help the teacher understand the values the student is likely to attach to particular learning opportunities, they may also suggest targets the teacher had not considered or had valued inappropriately. This interaction will not occur of its own accord, however. As I implied earlier, many parents do not see themselves as sufficiently knowledgeable to question the goals teachers have set for their children. Establishing the notion that such behavior is appropriate and welcome is important, and the demeanor of the teacher, who may also be threatened by such interaction, can determine how parents will behave. Yet unpublished research that Judy Gruber and I conducted in New Haven schools suggests that schools can encourage parental input by establishing parent-teacher councils at the school level with formal authority to participate constructively in decisions affecting what goes on in the classroom.

Interaction with Peers. A number of writers have pointed to the fact that teachers have little opportunity to interact professionally or to observe their peers and that this contributes to resistance to change.[31] Nevertheless, several studies show that their colleagues are the single most important source of information that teachers have about teaching.[32]

There are at least two requirements for fostering professional interaction among teachers: (1) time and structures that allow it to happen and (2) norms and established processes that reduce the personal costs and establish discussion of teaching problems and successes as a professional responsibility.

The contributions that interaction among peers are likely to make to adaptiveness probably increase proportionately with diversity within the interacting group.[33] At the same time, diversity may also cause work groups to fragment and communication to decline.

Administrators and Goal Setting. As indicated earlier, the clearer one's goals, the greater the likelihood of adaptive behavior. Administrators should therefore be concerned with assisting teachers, individually and collectively, to clarify and prioritize their own objectives and to specify goals for their students. Administrators who take this responsibility seriously will be in a position to facilitate interaction among teachers with similar objectives.

The comparison of the goals of the organization—or of its leadership—to those of a given teacher can be employed as a strategy to induce reconsideration of goals. The adjustment of an individual teacher's objectives can be encouraged by involving that teacher in key decisions concerning how resources are utilized and what curricula are adopted. When such involvement takes the form of group decision making, it is likely to facilitate a willingness to consider new alternative modes of behavior, assuming, of course, that the group is seeking answers to how the learning environment can be enhanced.

Relating Performance to Goals. The same processes of interaction that facilitate the consideration of alternative objectives and the sharpening of one's purposes also provide information on performance. Exchanges with administrators and peers provide the opportunity for subjective evaluation and interpersonal comparisons. These interactions, as well as those with students and parents and with professional information, encourage self-examination either by (1) raising the possibility that alternative ways of accomplishing certain objectives exist or (2) existing strategies are ineffective.[34]

But the most direct and perhaps most persuasive information on performance should come from objective evaluation of the teachers' contributions to the rate at which children in their classes develop cognitively and effectively. For such evaluation to be motivating, it must have at least two characteristics:

1. It must focus on the goals the teacher values.
2. The teacher must see the measures of performance upon which evaluation is based as adequate and appropriate.

If these two conditions are met, teachers are likely to take evaluations of their performance seriously since the two major rationalizations for dealing with dissonance that evaluation can cause are not available.

One can acquire information about performance from others or one can develop—and school systems can foster—the capacity to acquire the ability to assess themselves. Ronald Lippitt and his associates have argued that to encourage adaptive and innovative behavior, it is useful to:

... connect the teacher to the knowledge and methods of the behavioral sciences in order to enable him to conduct a personal research and development process in his classroom. For example, with some professional advice a teacher may administer a series of questionnaires or scientific instruments to his pupils. After analyzing and interpreting these data, he can derive a plan of action or innovation, test it out and evaluate it.[35]

Nonadaptiveness: An Offer One Can't Resist. It is possible that people can be induced to change their behavior not because they are unsatisfied with their performance or because they accept new goals urged on them by others but because their failure to change will bring about negative sanctions. But the capacity to induce a recognition of the need for adaptiveness in this way has clear limits.

Most of what a teacher does goes unobserved by supervisors or peers who might invoke sanctions. As the literature on innovation clearly shows, teachers enjoy considerable power to resist or substantially modify innovations they are directed to implement. Since it would seem that adherence to new programs or use of new materials is substantially easier to measure than adaptive behavior, the enforcement of demands that teachers adopt the latter is likely to be so great that negative sanctions will not be feared. This also means, of course, that the distribution of positive rewards for adaptiveness is difficult, a point I will return to.

Summary and Comment. This section argues that a predisposition to behave adaptively depends on the recognition that one is not performing to the standards one values. I have argued that in effect information-intensive school environments that focus their attention on the possibilities of new goals and/or new processes for achieving old goals foster adaptiveness.[36]

Fostering an awareness that progress toward the fulfillment of one's role expectations is possible is a motivational process similar to that which Argyris and others believe releases and sustains an individual's contribution of psychological energy to the attainment of organizational goals.[37] This process, of course, produces tension, and the stress a person experiences can lead to dysfunctional behavior and not to adaptiveness, depending on the individual's assessment of the relative costs and benefits he will incur in becoming and staying adaptive.

The higher the costs and the lower the benefits, the narrower the gaps should be between perception of one's present performance and one's expectations so that low morale, frustration, passivity, and other forms of counterproductive activity can be avoided. It is difficult to predict how wide the achievement gap should be to induce adaptive behavior; the ability of individuals to deal creatively with tension apparently varies with personality characteristics such as self-esteem, authoritarianism, and assertiveness.

Potential Costs of Adaptiveness

As noted earlier, adaptiveness requires the development of a repertoire of various approaches to teaching, the recurrent assessment of needs and capabilities of individual students, the selective application of techniques on an individual basis, the evaluation of the effectiveness of these techniques, and the reevaluation of one's abilities and the assessment of ways those abilities that need strengthening can be enhanced. The cost involved in achieving and maintaining such behavior can be thought of as technical and psychological.[38] Technical costs are those associated with the development and renewal of the ability to do these things. I use the term "psychological costs" here very loosely to include perceived loss of social esteem, status, and power, loss of self-esteem or self-confidence, frustration, and the like.

Technical Costs. Being adaptive requires the constant gathering and processing of new information. Moreover, since the needs and even the capacities of students change over time, the addition of new skills and the virtual retirement of others will be required.

Creating the rich information field necessary to provide a predisposition toward adaptiveness will reduce some search costs. Most teachers know a lot more about education than they do about other fields. Part of this is caused by time constraints, part of it is due to the fact that norms relating to information sharing are not firmly established, and part of the problem is that formal structures for multiperson problem solving are seldom extant. Administrators and teachers can learn to see themselves as resource people who, once aware of the needs and interests of individual teachers, can refer and provide materials to them. Within schools it seems possible to develop informal experts who acquire a reputation—and thus an incentive—for keeping people informed about their field.

Finally, adaptiveness may, though not necessarily, require new materials with which to work. The literature on educational innovation suggests that the adoption of innovation relates positively to the amount of fiscal resources available, though it may be that it is the *amount* of uncommitted resources rather than the total volume of uncommitted resources that is crucial.[39]

The hypothetical relationship between slack in a school system's fiscal resources and willingness to adopt innovations may also apply to the implementation of an innovation; however, empirical evidence is lacking. If such a linkage exists, it is because excess resources allow teachers to try new things that do cost money and to spend less time on scavenging instructional materials, which means that they can move on to thinking about enhancing learning environments.

Potential Psychological Costs. *Role Uncertainty.* People vary in their ability to tolerate ambiguity, but most of us seek to minimize uncertainty in our relationships with others and in our perception of our responsibilities. The absence of such definition can lead to internal tension and to group conflict.[40] In adaptive organizations tasks would be various, diffuse, and changing, while goals would often be multiple and general.

Responsibility. Adaptive organizations provide the individual with considerable autonomy but also with considerable responsibility for the attainment of organizational goals. If those working in hierarchical organizations do not achieve their objectives, they can always assign their failure to "the system" or to "constraints on my discretion" or directly to the principal. For example, teachers commonly explain the apparent "failure" of students in terms of the students' prior experience, other teachers, or the rigidities of the curriculum, and so on. When teachers play a central role in determining the character of the school and what goes on in the classroom, the "failure" of students to meet the teachers' expectations can be assigned only to students or to themselves. Often teachers feel the students' failure personally.

The willingness to act, particularly to take new initiatives, is related to one's sense of competence.[41] Thus broadening the scope and depth of one's responsibilities, even if desired by the worker, could result in a conservative approach to work and a sense of impotence. The more serious the individual believes the consequences of possible failure to be, the more likely that he will avoid coming to grips with the problems he faces. This avoidance of responsibility can take many forms. First, it may result in efforts to reduce autonomy by such means as centralizing authority, establishing standard operating procedures, and insisting on stronger leadership and in loss of professional confidence and self-esteem. Second, the avoidance of responsibility may make the worker focus only on those aspects of the jobs where success is most readily measured,[42] such as securing classroom discipline. This in turn may make quality control trivial and encourage adhering to routine, denying one's feelings, narrowing responsibility and specializing, transferring initiatives to others, and denying personal effectiveness.[43]

The "Problem" of High Aspirations and Identification with the Student. The opportunity to set one's goals, especially when high aspirations are first presented, often results in setting very ambitious targets, and the exhilaration that comes from being given significant responsibility may result in hopes for rapid and significant problem solving. If such high aspirations are disappointed, as they are likely to be, a sense of failure will invariably follow. Adaptiveness requires individual treatment of students which may lead to a heavy identification with students. Personalization of teaching coupled with excessive aspirations can lead to frustration and anxiety.

Professional Embarrassment. What teachers do in their classrooms is only vaguely known by other teachers. Deviant practices or special interests are generally known, but the nature of interaction with students goes largely unobserved and unreported. Adaptiveness, however, requires considerable interaction, frank discussion of problems, observation by others, and feedback on effectiveness. Though the last of these may never be public knowledge, depending on school policies, adaptiveness will "expose" teacher behavior to the scrutiny of others. Teachers who are least secure about their abilities and those who are in fact less effective may experience professional embarrassment.

Threats to Authority by Parents and Students. Teachers can assert authority and seek control of their classroom by denying the legitimacy of demands of others and by so structuring classroom events that acceptable student behavior is well defined and readily determinable. Adaptiveness requires that teachers grant parents and students the right to suggest objectives and question teaching strategies. This will increase some teachers' sense of vulnerability. Students in adaptive classrooms will see various standards and emphases applied to their peers and should experience less authoritarian behavior. Some students may interpret a teacher's responsiveness to student preferences and the opportunity to question why they are asked to do things as a breakdown in authority. Adaptive teachers do, in effect, surrender some power to students.

And, it seems likely, at least in the short run, that adaptiveness will undermine methods of student control employed in many so-called traditional classrooms.[44] Of course, if teaching effectiveness reduces disruption and purposeless behavior, adaptiveness will not be costly in this sense. Authority in this case will derive not from position per se but from the contributions teachers make to student development.

Social Disapproval. One of the most pervasive findings in the research on behavior is that the norms of the work group have enormous impact on the willingness of people to try new ideas. Limited evidence suggests that teachers as a group do not reward and may disapprove of peers who are innovators,[45] perhaps because innovations can disrupt the relative status of group members and bring about new external demands for changes in the behavior of everyone. Certainly, this negative predisposition is not pervasive, and whether or not it would be applied to adaptiveness is difficult to say. Adaptiveness allows a wide range of behavior to coexist so long as students benefit—which may seem less threatening than innovation.

Loss of Status or Power. The conditions necessary to attain adaptive schools will involve sharing authority and will, overall, involve a leveling up of status positions of individual teachers. This could mean that some teachers who enjoy special access to resources and information (because of their relations with administrators, contacts outside the school system, or the like) will lose status or power.[46] Department heads, master teachers, area coordinators, and even principals are likely to lose status and power relative to teachers.

Potential Benefits of Adaptiveness

Rewards Deriving from Effectiveness. I have previously made a case for the link between adaptive teaching and student learning. As I noted, there are good theoretical reasons to believe this link is strong. A sizeable body of school reform literature makes this argument in one way or another,[47] and there is also agreement among many students of school administration that organizational and individual adaptiveness facilitates good teaching. There is, however, only limited systematic evidence—in part because of the small number of schools studied that employ the type of open, collegial structures just described—that this is so.[48] But if, as Robert Schaefer suggests, a teacher is a diagnostician, a "stalker of meaning," and a constant learner, the importance of adaptiveness would be clear.[49]

Teachers benefit in several ways from their own effectiveness: (1) it enhances their self-confidence and self-esteem; (2) it is likely to bring social approval of colleagues; (3) it enhances the prestige of teaching among parents and other "lay persons"; (4) it carries the reward of having achieved a highly valued goal; and (5) it perhaps reduces tension between student and teachers and the likelihood of disruption.

All of this depends, of course, on the teachers' awareness of (or faith in) their own success,[50] and others' having knowledge of (or belief in) that success. This in turn depends on the nature of the evaluation system and the linkage of incentives to them. I will return to these very complex issues below.

A Reduction of Interpersonal Conflict over New Ideas. Almost all studies dealing with the implementation of innovations stress that group norms suppress the acceptance and use of new ideas.[51] Because adaptiveness requires reduction in status differences and extensive communication and interaction, one might expect the power of social norms and the costs of social disapproval to be lowest in least adaptive schools. But in adaptive schools, group norms will, as I have already suggested, focus on outcome rather than process or behavior. The result of this should be strong norms supporting experimentation and autonomy of style. This in turn should free teachers who value adaptiveness of some of the social disapproval of their deviance in approach. Unlike the innovation process, the success of which is often measured by how widely diffused and incorporated a given idea becomes, adaptiveness makes no such organizationwide demands.

Rewards Deriving from Structural Characteristics of Adaptive Schools. Adaptive schools will be characterized by certain organizational arrangements and leadership styles that I will outline in the next section. These characteristics offer rewarding opportunities over and above their impact on teaching effectiveness. Such opportunities include: (1) access to colleagues and social approval, (2) increases in one's role in decision making, and (3) professional discretion in the development of teaching approaches and classroom management.

Summary. I have argued that to attain adaptiveness in public schools, one must foster conditions that cause teachers to continually specify and reexamine their goals while providing them with evidence about their capacity to meet those objectives. But recognizing that one is falling short of one's goals and being aware that adaptiveness could improve teaching effectiveness will not necessarily cause one to behave adaptively. That commitment depends on the perceived costs and benefits of adaptiveness. I have tried to identify the sources of the costs and benefits and the factors that influence their magnitude.

Conclusion: Implications for the Organization and Administration of Schools

There are certain general implications of the foregoing analysis for how schools might be organized and for general directions that educational administration should take to secure maximum adaptiveness. As before, I have constrained this analysis to the motivational field that teachers experience directly, and the following discussion is also subject to that constraint. Important issues like the roles of school board politics, the impact of superintendents and their staffs, interorganizational competition, the incentives principals have to be adaptive, and the policies of other governments will go untouched here.

The Internal Structure of Adaptive Schools

The available literature suggests that organizational environments that are most effective in motivating people whose jobs require them to deal creatively with uncertainty and to respond flexibly and spontaneously to a variety of problem-solving demands generally provide these people with (1) a role in the development of organizational policies relevant to their work,[52] (2) some autonomy in setting individual goals and substantial freedom in determining the means to achieve those goals,[53] and (3) opportunities for professional interaction.[54]

It follows from these conclusions and from research on the traits of effective teachers,[55] that:

1. Adaptive schools should be organized collegially. Key decisions affecting teachers in general should be made democratically or *delegated* by teachers to decision makers.
2. Status differences within the school should be minimized, and formal differentiation of staff authority avoided.[56]
3. Organizational constraints on the individual behavior of teachers should be minimized but, when employed, be tied to linkages between behavior and teaching effectiveness.[57]

Guidelines for Leadership. It should be clear that conventional models of assertive, take-charge leadership are not appropriate to adaptive schools.[58] The leadership role should be that of the facilitator rather than coach or taskmaster. Facilitation of adaptive teaching would include emphasis on the following activities:

1. Attention should be given to goal clarification and specification and the relationship of goals to different teaching approaches.[59]

2. In-service training programs centered on the individual needs of teachers *as they define them* should be provided. Individual needs can of course be dealt with in group situations, but decisions by leaders on what people need to learn and the assignment of workers to designated programs will have few consequences for reducing anxiety and psychological stress.

3. Information on new ideas that relate to the goals teachers are pursuing should be provided.

4. The propensity to avoid goal specification and readjustment might be reduced if (a) leaders seek to identify differences in the objectives of individual group members and to raise questions about their compatibility, and (b) leaders foster continual feedback of both subjective and objective information about the capacity of *both* individuals and groups to meet their stated objectives. One relevant norm that leaders can develop in a group is the desirability of self-assessment and recurrent evaluation by peers. Another is the inherent value of individual input, and this norm is particularly important when there is status incongruence in the group. Finally, as Blau suggests, it is possible that organizations can develop ideological commitments to seek out and achieve new goals.[60] This can lead to the view that change is good in itself, but if emphasis is placed on the consequences of the change rather than rewarding changes in processes themselves, this problem may be controllable.

5. Norms encouraging participation in decision making should be fostered as should the notion that "different" ideas are valuable because they are different. E.P. Hollander, for example, found that in some organizations individuals could build up "idiosyncrasy credits," which facilitated deviant actions once basic loyalty to the group and its norms had been established.[61]

6. Efforts should be made to clarify the mutual dependence of specific teachers in terms of (a) shared responsibilities for particular students or (b) the interrelationships between the more general knowledge and experience students have.

7. Regular times should be set aside not only for group decision making but also for informal communication. Such discussions should involve only two or three members, and steps should be taken to rotate the members of such parlays.

8. Leaders should discourage the notion that they have the answer, however attractive it might be to be thought of as the source of wisdom. They should foster instead norms that support openness, the right and obligation of each member to observe and comment on the work of others, the distribution of leadership tasks to more than one member of the group, and the desirability of power sharing on an ad hoc basis.

9. As noted earlier, leaders need to manage the levels of tension that result from the identification of what I have called "performance gaps." But how? As Morton Deutsch observes, the results of studies dealing with the effects of tension are not definitive.[62] "The safest generalization seems to be that mild stress often improved group performance and increases cohesiveness while severe

stress often has the opposite effects." What is needed is what James March and Herbert Simon call "optimum stress."[63] The problem, of course, is to predict the point of diminishing returns. Among the factors that might determine how much stress can creatively be dealt with are: (a) the turbulence of the environment, (b) the self-confidence and cohesiveness of the group, (c) commitment to organizational goals by group members, (d) the nature of demands, (e) organizational resources (including teacher skills), and (f) the personalities of individual group members.

The Nature of Evaluation. Preceding pages have identified a number of reasons why evaluation of teaching performance is crucial to the attainment and maintenance of adaptiveness in public schools. Evaluation can be thought to have two major purposes: (1) to allow individuals and groups to improve their own performance and (2) to provide information to administrative superiors, policymakers, or clients that can be used to control or to impose change on the organization. Let me refer to the first of these purposes as *internal*, the second as *external.*

Both internal and external evaluations are difficult in school organizations precisely for the reasons that nonadaptiveness is important:

1. Organizational goals are often multiple and diffuse.
2. Knowledge about the best way to achieve organizational goals is not extensive or definitive.

Evaluation is not only difficult methodologically but it can also have significant costs to the organization. For example, to the extent it poses personal costs, it is likely to reduce risk taking and encourage adherence to familiar ways.[64] My objective is to suggest some guidelines for evaluation in adaptive schools aimed at maximizing relevant information about teacher performance and minimizing the potential costs such information and its gathering poses.

1. Internal evaluation of individuals seems best carried out and least likely to be resisted if rewards or sanctions are not directly associated with it. Such rewards or penalties are best administered by persons who are not members of the immediate organization or subunit.

This does not mean that adaptive organizations should not engage in evaluation; rather it means that the internal purposes of such activity should be to develop the capacity of individuals and the group to meet organizational goals. Can evaluation in the absence of formal sanctions induce change or otherwise motivate? The importance of social acceptance by peers and the desire most people seem to have for self-esteem should provide the appropriate leverage if the objectives involved are actually valued by the group or the individual. As noted earlier, the characteristics of adaptive schools are likely to encourage commitment to organizational goals. In any case, evaluation efforts should be individualized or at least tied to readily identified subgroups. Such a strategy would include the identification of individual or team objectives and the specific measures and types of evidence that group members agree are appropriate to know whether objectives they value have been achieved.

2. For purposes here, let me describe external evaluation as having political and administrative components. Political evaluation is aimed at holding the organization accountable for attaining specified objectives. Administrative evaluation, in addition to this function, concerns the control, advancement, or termination of individuals.

Political evaluation is usually the function of legislative or citizen bodies. It should be concerned solely with group performance—that is, the activity of the nonbureaucratic organization as a whole. The agents of political evaluation may, of course, collect their own data and deal directly with clients. Some of the information so collected may be relevant to assessing individual performance but would not be used externally. Administrators external to the nonbureaucratic work group should share the responsibility for monitoring group behavior.

3. A focus on the group, coupled with reluctance to punish short-run individual failure, may encourage the group itself to be concerned with contributing to goal-related effectiveness of its members. Moreover, there is evidence that individuals draw satisfaction from the success of the group which, in turn, encourages cohesion and collaboration.[65] And, emphasizing group performance in evaluation processes may provide a base from which intergroup competition can be induced. Administrative responsibility for personal evaluation in effect screens the individual from environmental threat. There are two reasons why this is important: (a) to encourage the individual to interact with clients and to develop task-related commitments outside the work group and (b) to facilitate evaluation of individuals over time in order to encourage personal growth and permit a time perspective that can reward adaptiveness in terms of long-term, rather than short-run, impact.

4. As noted earlier, the logic of adaptive schools will be undermined by evaluation that focuses on process rather than the development of students. Product objectives are those derived from organizational goals—as contrasted with various means that might be seen as advancing such goals.

5. If evaluation is to have developmental as well as judgmental purpose, members of the organization must be involved not only in goal setting, but also in the specification of performance criteria. Such criteria should ideally be subject to objective verification and should capture the range of organizational goals as well as their relative priority.

These several thoughts only scratch the surface of the difficulties of achieving an effective approach to evaluating adaptive teaching. In general, I have tried to stress the importance of maintaining high levels of feedback to the group and to individuals.

Direct Rewards for Adaptive Teaching. I have noted throughout that the potential motivational value of rewards for performance derives from leader and peer group approval, intrinsic satisfactions involved in achieving valued goals, and experiencing the working conditions necessary to maintaining adaptive organizations. But what is the role of material rewards and career advancement as incentives? Present reward structures in schools do not have much range, there is very limited room for advancement, and neither salary nor leadership roles seem to be closely tied to teaching performance as measured by what happens to students in particular schools or classrooms.

The issue that seems unresolved either by empirical studies[66] or theory is: Assuming one could measure performance, would the motivational value of such things as merit pay and differentiated staffing outweigh the costs with respect to personal conflict, poor communication, and low incentives for sharing skills and ideas? It does appear that ambitious teachers will adopt innovations in order to set themselves apart from others. And this entrepreneurship may result in the premature closure on innovations by other, less aggressive or less confident teachers.[67] How this relates to adaptiveness is uncertain. One possible but problematic way out of this dilemma is to reward people who excel in and commit themselves to processes that contribute to the success of others. This approach, however, has the peculiarity of focusing on process rather than product and perhaps rewarding people who are in fact less effective teachers.

Final Comments. Let me conclude by acknowledging two things. First, to secure adaptiveness initially may be thought of as an innovation. On the other hand, moving to a state of adaptiveness is likely to be an evolutionary and incremental process that is not easily packaged, which leads to the second point. Learning to be adaptive is no simple task and requires both the acquisition of technical and interpersonal skills on the one hand and the unlearning of certain behaviors on the other.

Following their extensive review of the literature, Harvey A. Averch and his colleagues offer the not very unique conclusion that a noticeable improvement of cognitive and noncognitive student outcomes "*may* require sweeping changes in the organization, structure and conduct of educational experience."[68]

While almost everyone agrees that educational change is necessary, research and policy seems to be guided by one or both of two assumptions: (1) there is one best way to teach particular subjects, and (2) schools that adopt innovations are more likely to be successful than those that do not. I have tried to suggest why these assumptions are misplaced and that before we worry about understanding the innovation process, we need to recognize that it, as well as teaching effectiveness, depends on understanding how schools can be made more adaptive. This recognition should stimulate experimentation and research, and I have attempted to suggest important considerations for both policymakers and students of education changefulness.

Comments

Paul T. Hill

Willis Hawley's paper identifies some of the chief sources of tension and confusion in American educational policy. His distinction between innovation (the imposition of new inventions in educational services, without serious thought about the needs of the particular students to be served) and adaptation (careful tailoring of services to meet clients' needs and aspirations) is a very useful one. However, I think Hawley's suggestions about how to achieve adaptive education miss the mark. They are based on the assumption that schools will become adaptive if teachers and principals learn to value adaptation. Yet many of the pressures for innovation and against adaptation come from outside the school. Those pressures will not slacken at all in response to the in-school reforms that Hawley suggests.

I would like to achieve two things in my comments. The first is to argue that the concern for innovation pervades the whole educational system and that correctives at the school level are unlikely to succeed. The second is to identify some prerequisites to adaptive education and briefly to suggest the outlines of research that might help bring it about.

Systemic Forces for Innovation

My first theme is that innovation is a deeply rooted preoccupation of the American educational system and that correctives must not stop at the school level but instead address the systemic causes. Hawley has argued very convincingly that services invented at one level are unlikely to be faithfully implemented or effective at another. Unfortunately, such an argument is not enough to discourage inventors from trying to control educational systems so their innovations can be tried. Despite over ten years of unhappy experience with innovation, the pressure to invent new services and to have government mandate their use is undiminished.

The pressure to innovate is partly the result of confusion about the roles of different levels of government in the educational process. Though only local educational agencies deliver educational services, the federal and state governments eagerly assume responsibility for the quality and success of instructional services.

The main federal program for aid to elementary and secondary education, ESEA Title I, is a case in point. Though the legislation permits school districts to use funds in a variety of ways, and less than half the funds are invested in reading instruction, still the U.S. Office of Education relies on reading test-score changes as its criterion for the success of the program. Evaluators have pursued evidence that Title I raises reading test scores in the sincere belief that that alone can justify continuing the federal investment. Many state education agencies have adopted similar positions toward their own compensatory education programs.

Only profound confusion about the roles of higher levels of government could support anyone's believing that a program as diverse and permissive as Title I should be regarded as a machine for producing test-score gains. That belief, however, is consistent with the fact that people at all levels of the educational hierarchy are encouraged to think of themselves essentially as teachers, whose only concern is with the effects of their actions on students. Teachers may regard this as a redundant role for state and federal officials to play, and they are right. But, given the professional backgrounds of federal and state education agency staff, the confusion about roles is easy to understand.

In the ten-year period since the large-scale establishment of federal aid to education, the staffing of the American educational system has changed in a way that reinforces the pressure for innovation. Federal, state, and local education agencies are now dominated by people with advanced training in curriculum design and program evaluation. A major share of all the regulation writing, monitoring, verification, and administration (and a considerable amount of teaching) is now done by people who have or aspire to doctorates from schools of education. Despite differences in the formal roles they occupy, all are primarily interested in affecting the services that schools deliver to students. It should be no surprise that a policy system staffed by such people will be marked by conflict over who is to design and evaluate educational services. To a great extent, educational policy is made through a struggle among potential curriculum innovators, with each trying for autonomy from innovators above and control over innovators below. Would-be innovators seek the support of Congress, the federal and state offices of education, and interest groups to get their inventions mandated into practice. Teachers ultimately control their own classrooms, and generally do not need higher authorities to mandate the services they prefer. But teachers too can become innovators in the negative sense of Hawley's term, if they invent new services without carefully assessing their students' needs. Clearly, adaptive education is not simply teacher-controlled education, and teachers who innovate out of a desire for professional self-expression are just another element of the system's pressure to innovate.

Though the struggle among potential innovators is usually conducted in the languages of educational philosophy and social science theory, the real concern of the participants is to exercise the professional role for which they were trained, i.e., to design and evaluate classroom instructional services. In the long run, the exact nature of services to be delivered is negotiated among the contending innovators, with too little attention to the needs and aspirations of students and their parents.

Even if teachers and principals learned to value adaptive approaches to education, the systemwide pressures for innovation would remain. Schools would still have to struggle for autonomy against "outside innovators." In short, the pressures for innovation would not diminish at all.

Capacities Necessary for Adaptive Education

To conclude, as I have just done, that the system must change is surely one of the most inane actions in the repertoire of policy analysis. Yet it is necessary in the face of Hawley's suggestion that a systemic problem can be treated successfully at the school level, through the careful nurturance of teachers. Such a suggestion implies that the system has the capacity to be adaptive, if only practitioners were properly motivated. I think, to the contrary, that few schools or educational systems have the capacity to be adaptive. The second part of my comment will try to identify some capacities that educational systems must have if they are to provide adaptive education and suggest lines of research that may make the changes possible.

Improved Accountability Systems. The first such capacity concerns federal and state educational agencies. They must develop a new system of accountability so that schools can be adaptive while giving funding agencies solid assurance that money is being used legally. The second capacity affects federal, state, and local education agencies, all of which need to direct the professional incentives of their administrative staffs away from innovating on classroom instructional services and toward supporting schools' and teachers' efforts to provide adaptive programs. The third capacity affects schools, which need ways of determining their clients' educational needs so that services can be adapted to them.

The first prerequisite is a system of accountability whereby those who deliver educational services can be adaptive to their clients, yet assure higher levels of management that funds are used for the general purposes for which they were appropriated. Teachers and local administrators are quite articulate about the negative effects of federal and state regulations that control the time, place, and manner of instruction.

Yet there is another side to the issue. It is that social service programs (in housing, health, etc., as well as education) tend to lose their programmatic character if funding agencies do not make explicit requirements of local practitioners. D.O. Porter has documented the case nicely for school districts' use of federal aid funds.[69] Paul E. Peterson's review of community action agency programs[70] and my own work on the Office of Economic Opportunity (OEO) home-ownership programs[71] conclude that service deliverers become innovators very readily and serve different clients with quite different services than were originally intended. In the OEO experience, service deliverers often became one-person, comprehensive social-service agencies, providing aid of all kinds to people who were identified through patronage or other informal processes. Whatever one thinks of general social work on behalf of needy individuals, that is clearly not the intent of categorical federal or state education programs. (And, likewise, whatever one thinks about whether teachers or administrators should control instruction, teacher sovereignty is no more likely to guarantee adaptive education than is the current system.) Educational programs are not popular enough with Congress and state legislatures to be proof against the inevitable journalistic exposés about the idosyncratic use of funds by local providers on behalf of a haphazardly selected population.

A new system of accountability—one that permits principals and teachers to be adaptive while assuring higher levels of government that funds are used to provide real educational services to the beneficiaries identified by law—is clearly needed.

There may be no such thing in this country as a strict accountability system for the use of educational funds. But accountability is now attempted, through two basic methods. The first is central management. It uses fiscal monitoring, on-site verification, and financial sanctions, all conducted by the funding agency. This is approximately the system used by the U.S. Office of Education for ESEA Title I and other programs of assistance for elementary and secondary education. Though simple in conception, the central management method is extremely hard to follow in intergovernmental relations. State education agencies play ambivalent roles in the management of Title I, acting sometimes as agents of U.S. Office of Education and other times as protectors of the school districts. And the school districts themselves are too numerous (over 14,000 in Title I) to permit direct management by the Office of Education or the states. As a result, the "direct-management" method has become a loose framework of regulations that require Local Education Agencies to report that they are using funds in specified ways. Reports that are "in compliance" may mask misuse of funds, just as reports "out of compliance" may reflect the efforts of an LEA to meet local needs in just the way that Title I's congressional authors intended. Still, given the size and complexity of the federal system, the current accountability system for federal education programs may be about as effective as it can be.

The second method is accountability by results. This removes funding agencies entirely from the business of monitoring program administration and rewards or punishes LEAs and schools solely on their students' achievement gains. This method was so popular in the early 1970s that it came under the kinds of intense critical scrutiny that is usually reserved for frontrunners in presidential primary races. Critics noted that funding LEAs on the basis of positive results hurts the students most in need (i.e., those whose school systems are serving them least well). Politicians noted the same thing: Michigan's celebrated accountability system was amended when big-city LEAs were about to lose funding. All of which calls into question whether accountability systems based on reading and mathematics achievement test results hold education agencies responsible for the outcomes that the ultimate funding agencies, i.e., Congress and the state education agencies, are really most concerned about. Quite clearly the Michigan legislature was more concerned about keeping Detroit's school system operating than about the niceties of student achievement test results. The same is true of Congress, which has increased support of Title I despite the Office of Education's difficulty in linking Title I spending with students' gains on reading and mathematics achievement tests. Continuing to support educational programs despite poor test results is not a sign of lost political nerve, but evidence that the accountability criterion is not exactly what legislators had in mind in the first place.

These two methods of accountability need considerable refinement. In the case of central management, it is time to look seriously at the problems of central management in an intergovernmental context. It is now easy to identify the shortcomings of federal educational management, but for all we know the central management method may already have reached its technical limits. In the case of accountability by results, it is clear that the most commonly used outcome criterion does not reflect legislators' concerns; until such a criterion is devised, accountability by results can only be a slogan. The whole topic of accountability needs a serious review in order to understand the degree to which the two methods outlined above can permit schools to be adaptive while ensuring funding agencies that funds are used properly. A natural topic for such a review would be the potential of hybrid methods, which combine elements of central management, accountability by results, and other techniques. In light of the concern for adaptiveness, one promising "other technique" is accountability through local enforcement whereby local advocacy groups are responsible for the on-site verification that central managers cannot do. Federal and state education programs now contain the seeds of such a management technique in the form of local parent advisory councils, but the technique requires very serious prior research and planning.

Changed Incentives for Administrators. The second prerequisite of adaptive schooling is a change in the structure of professional incentives for educational administrators. As long as educational administrators find true professional fulfillment by competing with teachers for control of classrooms, adaptive education will be impossible.

Such a change in incentives will be hard to bring about without sacrificing the creativity and vigor that has resulted from the increased professionalism of educational managers. The solution is not to hire managers who are less knowledgeable about education, but to redefine their roles so that they complement, rather than compete with, teachers and principals.

The federal government is uniquely equipped to provide funds for education programs and to manage and finance very expensive research into learning. On the other hand, the federal government can do very little about the details of the selection and delivery of educational services. The same is true of the states, whose natural role vis-à-vis instructional services may be dissemination and technical assistance (but not innovation!). By elimination, this leaves local practitioners to select and implement services, with specific kinds of help available from federal and state experts. Such a division of roles is so obvious that it must be forthcoming, as administrators adjust to the fact that they are really not deliverers of educational services. For the future, schools of education might add state and federal program management to the research and training agendas of future professionals.

A Way of Assessing Clients' Needs. The third prerequisite for adaptive education is a way for professionals to discover what they must adapt to. A major shortcoming of Hawley's paper is its assumption that schools can readily discover what their clients' needs are. Consistent with that assumption, Hawley advocates the use of diagnostic-prescriptive instructional strategies, which are based on standard typologies of educational objectives and come packaged with instruments for measuring students' progress. Such techniques do make teachers more aware of their students, but they do not guarantee adaptive schooling. In fact, they establish systems of educational objectives that researchers and teachers, not students or parents, have invented. These objectives may fit local needs and aspirations nicely, but then they may not. Recent efforts to understand parents' aspirations for their children's schooling have shown that parents have strong views but find it difficult to express them. Research about lay participation in school policymaking gives a discouraging picture of laymen's ability to make clear and effective presentation of their demands for educational services. Zeigler[72] and others have shown that school boards and other lay advisory groups serve largely to ratify professional choices. More recent research on Title I parent advisory councils suggest that their role too is marginal. At best, the councils select from short lists of alternatives formulated by professionals.

The need for a way of discovering parents' and students' aspirations for education is clear. Yet formal decision-making bodies are too intimidating to parents, and standard survey approaches almost always rely on questions formulated in advance by teachers and educational researchers; they may or may not tap the areas of local clients' greatest concern about education.

The best natural device for communicating lay clients' aspirations is a free and functionally perfect market, which allows clients to make an infinite variety of concrete choices. That clearly does not exist in education because reforms like vouchers and free schools offer too few alternatives to permit truly effective market choices. As long as educational services are packaged and delivered by a few large institutions, there will be a need for articulation of clients' aspirations so that adaptive programs can be provided.

If clients cannot spontaneously make a full statement of their goals for education, perhaps some artificial device can facilitate it. Such a device would have to help clients to scan their expectations broadly and to express them in terms that the professionals who run educational institutions can understand.

The National Institute of Education (NIE) has supported a three-year research program to develop a simple method whereby school officials can assess their clients' aspirations for educational services. Early results indicate that parents in particular have different priorities for some educational outcomes than teachers and that some topics that preoccupy teachers do not concern parents at all. Further results in the form of a report by P.J. Blackwell and L.S.

Smith will be available in late 1976.[73] That work may point the way toward taking serious account of clients' needs and aspirations and thus help provide agendas for adaptive schooling.

Conclusion

I can only conclude by endorsing Hawley's analysis of the importance of adaptive education; yet I must insist that his prescriptions are too modest. My chief complaint against the paper is that it looks only within the school for solutions to the school's problems. In so doing, the paper has failed to recognize the paradox that today's educational policy research can help the schools only if it looks beyond them, to the structure and incentives of the whole educational system.

Notes

1. This set of ideas follows those of Robert P. Biller, "Adaption Capacity and Organizational Development," in *Toward a New Public Administration: The Minnowbrook Perspective*, ed. Frank Marini (Scranton, Penn.: Chandler, 1971), p. 113.

2. Matthew B. Miles and D.G. Lake, "Self-Renewal in School Systems: A Strategy for Planned Change," in *Concepts for Social Change*, ed. George E. Watson (Washington, D.C.: COPED by NTL, NEA, 1967), p. 82.

3. Cf. Murray J. Edelman, *The Symbolic Uses of Politics* (Urbana, Ill.: University of Illinois Press, 1964).

4. Of course, education does not have a corner on unsuccessful innovations. See, for example, Frederick Mosteller, "Comments on 'The Value of Social Experiments,' " in *Planned Variation in Education: Should We Give Up or Try Harder*, eds., Alice M. Rivlin and P. Michael Timpane (Washington, D.C.: The Brookings Institution, 1975), pp. 169-172.

5. Almost all the research measures effectiveness in terms of cognitive development. See M.J. Wargo, P.L. Campeau, and G.K. Tallmadge, *Further Examination of Exemplary Programs for Educating Disadvantaged Children* (Palo Alto, Calif.: American Institute for Research, 1971); The Ford Foundation, *A Foundation Goes to School: The Ford Foundation Comprehensive School Improvement Program 1960-1970* (New York: Office of Reports, Nov. 1972); N.L. Gage, ed. *Handbook of Research on Teaching* (Chicago, Ill.: Rand McNally, 1963); J.M. Stephens, *The Process of Schooling* (New York: Holt, Rinehart and Winston, 1967); Robert M.W. Travers, *Second Handbook of Research on Technology* (Skokie, Ill.: Rand McNally, 1973); Harvey A. Averch et al., *How Effective Is Schooling?: A Critical Review and Synthesis of Research*

Findings (Santa Monica, Calif.: The Rand Corporation, 1972); Westinghouse Learning Corporation/Ohio University, *The Impact of Head Start: An Evaluation of the Effects of Head Start Experience on Children's Cognitive and Affective Development* (Springfield, Va.: Clearinghouse for Federal Scientific and Technical Information, U.S. Department of Commerce, June 12, 1969); U.S. Office of Education, *Statistical Report Fiscal Year 1968: A Report on the Third Year of Title I Elementary and Secondary Education Act of 1965* (Washington, D.C.: U.S. Government Printing Office, 1970); Gene Glass, *Data Analysis of the 1968-69 Survey of Compensatory Education (Title I), Final Report* (Boulder, Colo.: Laboratory of Educational Research, University of Colorado, Aug. 1970); Milbrey Wallin McLaughlin, *Education and Reform: The Elementary and Secondary Educational Act of 1965, Title I* (Cambridge, Mass.: Ballinger, 1975). Focusing on cognitive development, as most studies do, may also understate the importance of innovations to changing school outcomes. This conclusion is the thrust of the argument offered by Lyn S. Martin and Barbara V. Pavan in their review of the research on the impact of new approaches to teaching and classroom structuring. See Martin and Pavan, "Current Research on Open Space, Nongrading, Vertical Grouping and Teaching," *Phi Delta Kappan* 57 (Jan. 1976): 310-315.

6. Martin and Pavan, "Current Research."

7. Averch et al., *How Effective is Schooling?*, p. 151.

8. Cf. Rivlin and Timpane, eds. *Planned Variation in Education*, 1975.

9. Paul Berman and Milbrey Wallin McLaughlin, *Federal Programs Supporting Educational Change, Vol. II: The Findings in Review* (Santa Monica, Calif.: The Rand Corporation, 1974).

10. Matthew B. Miles, ed., *Innovation in Education* (New York: Bureau of Publications, Teachers College, Columbia University, 1964).

11. John I. Goodlad, "The Schools vs. Education," *Saturday Review* (April 19, 1961): 60.

12. See Marshall S. Smith, "Evaluation Findings in Head Start Planned Variation," in *Planned Variation in Education*, eds. Rivlin and Timpane, pp. 101-112; and Paul Berman and Milbrey Wallin McLaughlin, *Federal Programs Supporting Educational Change*, Vol. IV.

13. Averch et al., *How Effective is Schooling?*, p. 149.

14. Cf. Charles C. Jung, Robert Fox, and Ronald Lippitt, "An Orientation and Strategy for Working on Problems of Change in School Systems," in *Change in School Systems*, ed. Gordon Watson (Washington, D.C.: NEA National Training Laboratories, 1967), p. 69.

15. Charles C. Jung, Robert Fox, and Ronald Lippitt, "An Orientation and Strategy for Working on Problems of Change in School Systems," in *Change in School Systems*, ed. Gordon Watson (Washington, D.C.: NEA National Training Laboratories, 1967), p. 69.

16. Winfred F. Hill, "Learning Theory," *Encyclopedia of Education*, 10 vols. (New York: Macmillan, 1971), 5:471.

17. Norma Furst and Russell A. Hill, "Systematic Classroom Observation," *Encyclopedia of Education*, 2:181. On the same point, see David R. Krathwohl, "Cognitive and Affective Learning," ibid., p. 198; and David W. Ecker, "Affective Learning," ibid., 1:114.

18. Norman E. Wallen and Robert M.W. Travers, "Analysis and Investigation of Teaching Methods" in *Handbook of Research on Teaching*, ed. N.L. Gage (Chicago: Rand McNally, 1963), p. 500. The absence of empirically based theories of instruction is the recurrent theme of over half the articles on teaching collected recently by Ronald Hyman under the title *Contemporary Thought on Teaching* (Englewood Cliffs, N.J.: Prentice-Hall, 1971).

19. Averch et al., *How Effective is Schooling?*

20. Ibid., p. 119. (Cf. also p. 149.)

21. One reason the research does not take us very far in this regard is that very few studies actually measure the variation of what teachers actually do in the classroom regardless of the processes they or others say are experienced by students. No large-scale studies, and these have received the most attention, monitor teacher behavior.

22. David R. Krathwohl, "Cognitive and Affective Learning," *Encyclopedia of Education*, 4:156.

23. Cf. David G. Ryan, *Characteristics of Teachers: Their Description, Comparison and Appraisal* (Washington, D.C.: American Council on Education, 1960); Norman A. Sprinthall, John M. Whitely, and Ralph L. Mosher, "A Study of Teacher Effectiveness," *Journal of Teacher Education* 17 (Spring 1966): 93-106; and Philip Jackson, *Life in Classrooms* (New York: Holt, Rinehart, and Winston, 1968), chap. 4.

24. Joseph B. Giacquinta, "The Process of Organizational Change in Schools," in *Review of Educational Research*, Vol. 1, ed. Frederick N. Kerlinger (Itasca, Ill.: F.E. Peacock, 1974), p. 178. Similar conclusions are reached by other reviews of the literature; cf. Berman and McLaughlin, *Federal Programs Supporting Educational Change, Vol. I: A Model of Educational Change* (Santa Monica, Calif.: The Rand Corporation, 1974).

25. Berman and McLaughlin, *Federal Programs Supporting Educational Change, Vol. IV: The Findings in Review* (Santa Monica, Calif.: The Rand Corporation, 1975).

26. An example is federal programming with respect to innovation in reading. See Miles Myers, "Uncle Sam's Reading Puppeteer," *Learning* 4 (November 1975): 20-27.

27. Berman and McLaughlin, *Federal Programs Supporting Educational Change, Vol. I*; cf. Averch et al., *How Effective is Schooling?*

28. Cf. Lloyd A. Rowe and William B. Boise, "Organizational Innovation: Current Research and Evolving Concepts," *Public Administration Review* 34 (May/June 1974): 287; and Giacquinta, "The Process of Organizational Change in Schools."

29. Berman and McLaughlin, *Federal Programs Supporting Educational Change, Vol. I*, p. 8 ff.

30. The importance of professional involvement of teachers to innovation is found by Ronald G. Corwin, "Innovation in Organizations: The Case of Schools," *Sociology of Education* 48 (Winter 1975): 1-37.

31. Willis D. Hawley, "Dealing with Organizational Rigidity in Public Schools: A Theoretical Approach," and D.E. Tope, "Summary of Seminar on Change Processes in Public Schools," in *Change Processes in Public Schools*, ed. Richard O. Carlson (Eugene, Ore.: The Center for Advanced Study of Educational Administration, University of Oregon, 1965).

32. This research is reviewed concisely by Ernest House, *The Politics of Educational Innovation* (Berkeley, Calif.: McCutchan, 1974), pp. 70-73.

33. Cf. Jerald Hage and Michael Aiken, *Social Change in Complex Organizations* (New York: Random House, 1970); and Corwin, "Organizational Innovation: The Case of Schools," p. 31.

34. One study of 176 sixth-grade classrooms found that student responses to questionnaires about teacher behavior could be used to change teachers' behavior when the answers brought attention to the fact that teachers' images of what they were doing were different from those of their students. N.L. Gage, Philip J. Runkel, and B.B. Chatteridge, "Changing Behavior through Feedback from Pupils: An Application of Equilibrium Theory," in *Readings in the Social Psychology of Education*, eds. W.W. Charters, Jr., and N.L. Gage (Boston: Allyn and Bacon, 1963), pp. 173-181.

35. Ronald Lippitt et al., "The Teacher as Innovator, Seeker and Sharer of New Practices," in *Perspectives on Educational Change*, ed. Richard Miller (New York: Appleton-Century-Crofts, 1967), p. 309.

36. There is almost unanimous agreement among writers on educational change that information-intensive schools are more likely to be innovative than those in which internal communication, environmental feedback, and knowledge about professional developments are weak. This applies to all stages of the innovation process. Such conclusions, however, rest heavily on research in public organizations other than schools and on the work of various organization theorists. See, for example, Rowe and Boise, "Organizational Innovation: Current Research."

37. Cf. Chris Argyris, *Integrating the Organization and the Individual* (New York: Wiley, 1964).

38. Other kinds of costs are conceivable but not likely. Being adaptive

could result in the loss of material rewards only if performance were tied to rewards and adaptiveness led to decreasing effectiveness. For reasons set out previously, these possibilities are remote.

39. Matthew B. Miles argues that adoption of innovations is related to the availability of material supports. "Innovation in Education: Some Generalizations," in *Innovation in Education*, ed. Matthew B. Miles (New York: Bureau of Publications, Teachers College, Columbia University, 1964), pp. 635-639. See also Rowe and Boise, "Organizational Innovation: Current Research," p. 289.

40. Cf. Neal C. Gross et al., *Explorations in Role Analysis* (New York: Wiley, 1958); and R.K. Merton, "The Role Set: Problems in Sociological Theory," *British Journal of Sociology* 8 (1958): 106-120.

41. Cf. Argyris, *Integrating the Organization and the Individual*; and Victor H. Broom, *Work and Motivation* (New York: Wiley, 1964).

42. J.D. Thompson, *Organizations in Action* (New York: McGraw-Hill, 1967), pp. 120-122.

43. I.E.P. Menzies, "A Case-study in the Functioning of Social Systems as a Defence Against Anxiety," *Human Relations* 13 (1960): 95-121; and Michael Lipsky, "Street Level Bureaucracy and the Analysis of Urban Reform," *Urban Affairs Quarterly* 6 (1971): 391-410.

44. Sieber observes that innovations that help teachers manage their environments, including keeping children under control, are the most readily accepted. S.D. Sieber, "Organizational Influences on Innovative Roles," in *Knowledge Production and Utilization in Educational Administration*, eds. T.L. Edell and J.M. Kitchel (Eugene, Ore.: Center for the Advanced Study of Educational Administration, University of Oregon, 1968).

45. See Edwin M. Bridges, "The Principal and the Teachers: The Problem of Organizational Change," in *Perspectives on the Changing Role of the Principal*, ed. Richard W. Saxe (Springfield, Ill.: Thomas, 1968), pp. 62-63 and the sources cited there.

46. There is some evidence that loss of status or fear thereof is associated with opposition to innovation in schools. M.S. Atwood, "Small Scale Administrative Change: Resistance to the Introduction of a High School Guidance Program," in *Innovation in Education*, ed. Matthew B. Miles; Richard O. Carlson, "Unanticipated Consequences in the Use of Programmed Instruction," in *Adoption of Educational Innovations*; Lippitt et al., "The Teacher as Innovator, Seeker and Sharer of New Practices"; and Joseph B. Giacquinta, "Status Risk and Receptivity to Innovations in Complex Organizations: A Study of Responses of Four Groups of Educators to the Proposed Introduction of Sex Education in Elementary School," *Sociology of Education* 48 (Winter 1975): 38-58.

47. Cf. Averch et al., *How Effective Is Schooling?*, pp. 126-147 and the sources cited there.

48. See Jackson, *Life in Classroom*, chap. 4; Norman A. Sprinthall, John M. Whitely, and Ralph L. Mosher, "A Study of Teacher Effectiveness," *Journal of Teacher Education* 17 (Spring 1966): 93-106; and Wayne J. Doyle, "Effects of Achieved Status of Leaders on the Productivity of Groups," *Administrative Science Quarterly* 16 (March 1971): 40-50.

49. See Robert Shaefer, *The School as a Center of Inquiry* (New York: Harper & Row, 1967), p. 57.

50. The literature on innovativeness supports the not surprising notion that innovations have a greater chance of adoption to the extent that potential adaptors see them as improving a teacher's chances of achieving valued goals. See, for example, E.M. Rogers and F.F. Shoemaker, *Communication of Innovations* (New York: Free Press, 1971).

51. For example, after reviewing the literature, Ernest House observed that "there is a strong tendency for group values to turn reorientations [innovations] into variations and variations into regular practice" (*The Politics of Educational Innovation*, p. 77). See also Giacquinta, "The Process of Organizational Change in Schools," p. 189.

52. Daniel Katz and Robert Kahn, *The Social Psychology of Organizations* (New York: Wiley, 1966), p. 426; Chris Argyris, "Organizational Effectiveness," *International Encyclopedia of the Social Sciences*, 17 vols. (New York: Macmillan and Free Press, 1968), 11:317 and the sources cited there; and Ronald Havelock, *Planning for Innovation*, pp. 6, 33. It may be noted that participation in the identification of organizational or group objectives and power sharing in general results in greater commitment to the attainment of such goals (Katz and Kahn, p. 332) and to consensus over goals, resulting in organizational effectiveness (Smith and Ari, 1968).

53. Katz and Kahn, *The Social Psychology of Organizations*, p. 362; Robert J. House et al., "Relation of Leader Consideration and Initiating Structure to R and D Subordinates' Satisfaction," *Administrative Science Quarterly* 16 (March 1971): 19-30; Martin Patchen, *Participation, Achievement and Involvement on the Job* (Englewood Cliffs, N.J.: Prentice-Hall, 1970); Frederick Herzberg, *Work and the Nature of Man* (Cleveland: World Publishing, 1966); and Chris Argyris, *Integrating the Organization and the Individual*, chaps. 3, 8, 9 especially. Edwin Bridges has argued that teachers resist innovation because its imposition from "above" is seen as a violation of professional status: "The Principal and the Teachers: The Problem of Organizational Change," in *Perspectives on the Changing Role of the Principal*, ed. Richard Saxe (Springfield, Ill.: Thomas, 1968), p. 63.

54. Donald C. Pelz, "The Innovating Organization: Conditions for Innovation," and Chris Argyris, *Integrating the Organization and the Individual*. Opportunities for interpersonal interaction with co-workers increases job satisfaction (Sawatsky, 1941; Richards and Dobryns, 1957) and, when interaction is

related to the attainment of organizational goals, also increases productivity (Bass, 1960: 51-53).

55. Andrew Halpin, *Theory and Research in Administration* (New York: Macmillan, 1966), chap. 4; Arthur F. Corey, "Overview of Factors Affecting the Holding Power of the Teaching Profession," in *The Teacher Dropout*, ed. Timothy M. Stinnett (Itasca, Ill.: F.E. Peacock, 1970), pp. 2-3, 8-9; Philip Jackson, *Life in Classrooms*, chap. 4; Sarason, *The Culture of the School and the Problem of Change* (Boston: Allyn & Bacon, 1970), p. 169.

56. Elizabeth Cohen has found, for example, that equal-status teacher groups allow greater feelings of influence and job satisfaction and provide more chances for rewards from peers: Cohen, "Open-Space Schools: The Opportunity to Become Ambitious," *Sociology of Education* 46 (Spring 1973): 143-161.

57. As I have already implied, research on the structural characteristics of innovative organizations seems to offer up conflicting evidence. Some writers believe, for example, that innovation is facilitated by centralization, and others conclude that decentralization enhances the adoption and implementation of new programs. It may be, as Lippitt and his associates and Shepard imply, that teacher-initiated innovation is more likely in decentralized and less structured schools while those in charge of centralized and hierarchical schools are in a better position to impose programs developed elsewhere. Teacher-generated innovation is one aspect of adaptiveness that suggests the importance of autonomy to adaptive teaching. This research is succinctly reviewed by Ronald G. Corwin, "Innovation in Organizations: The Case of Schools," pp. 6-7. Corwin also cites studies showing that innovation is often impeded by formal, hierarchical organizational structures.

58. The literature on innovation suggests that directive leadership is associated with both (1) formal adoption of innovations and (2) weak implementation and incorporation of the change. See Sieber, "Organizational Influences on Innovative Roles."

59. The importance of this function is emphasized and discussed by Hawley, "Dealing with Organizational Rigidity in Public Schools"; and Giacquinta, "The Process of Organizational Change in Schools," p. 196.

60. P. Blau, *The Dynamics of Bureaucracy* (Chicago: University of Chicago Press, 1955).

61. E.P. Hollander, "Competence and Conformity in the Acceptance of Influence," *Journal of Abnormal and Social Psychology* 61 (1960): 365-369.

62. Morton Deutsch, "Groups: Group Behavior," *International Encyclopedia of the Social Sciences* 6:272.

63. James G. March and Herbert A. Simon, *Organizations* (New York: Wiley, 1958), p. 154.

64. On this point with reference to the potentially stifling effect that

accountability may have on innovation, see David P. Weikert and Barnard A. Banet, "Model Design Problems in Follow Through," in *Planned Variation in Education*, ed. Rivlin and Timpane, pp. 61-78. Hage and Aiken (*Social Change in Complex Organizations*) argue that conditions increasing the rate of organizational change include lower emphases on the volume and efficiency of production.

65. D.M. Shaw, "Size of Share in Task and Motivation Groups," *Sociometry* 23 (1960): 203-208.

66. For example, studies disagree on the relative importance of material versus other incentives for inducing teachers to adopt and implement innovations. Cf. Thomas Stephens, "Innovative Teaching Practices: Their Relation to System Norms and Rewards," *Educational Administration Quarterly* 10 (Winter 1974): 35-43; and Dennis W. Spuck, "Reward Structures in the Public High School," *Educational Administration Quarterly* 10 (Winter 1974): 18-34.

67. Ernest House, *The Politics of Educational Innovation*, chap. 4.

68. Averch et al., *How Effective is Schooling?*, p. x (emphasis added).

69. D.O. Porter, *The Politics of Budgeting Federal Aid: Resource Mobilization by Local School Districts* (Beverly Hills, Calif.: Sage Publications, 1973).

70. Paul E. Peterson, "Forms of Representation: Participation of the Poor in the Community Action Program," *American Political Science Review* (June 1970): 491-507.

71. P.T. Hill, "Home Ownership and the Poor," a publication of the Department of Housing and Urban Development's National Housing Subsidy Study, 1973.

72. L. Harmon Zeigler, "The Responsiveness of Public Schools to their Clientele," report of The Center for the Advanced Study of Educational Administration (Eugene, Ore., University of Oregon), 1973.

73. P.J. Blackwell, and L.S. Smith, "The Final Report of the NIE Educational Goals Study," unpublished, 1976.

Professionalism, Community Structure, and Decision-making School Superintendents and Interest Groups

2

Michael O. Boss,*
Harmon Zeigler,
Harvey Tucker,
and L.A. Wilson II

Experts and Group Conflict

The political influence of technological élites has captured the imagination of social scientists, and for good reason.[1] In a technological age, especially one in which the conservation of scarce resources replaces the distribution of abundant resources as a focus of policy, elected officials are frequently required to deal with issues containing components too sophisticated for them to comprehend. Thus they turn to experts for information, and the experts' knowledge is easily transformed into a political resource for the acquisition of influence. Recognition of the growing importance of experts has caused social scientists to reevaluate their empirical and normative models of public policy formation.

Traditional democratic theory holds that political influence follows—and ought to follow—lines of legal authority. The public elects a representative legislative body (congress, city council, school board) to make policy. An executive body, whose senior officials are elected or appointed, is employed to administer policy. Administrators follow the instructions of legislators, who follow the instructions of their constituents, communicated either individually or collectively. The major source of power is popular electoral and organizational support, and the norm of policy decision making is responsiveness to public desires and preferences. The newer model, what might be called the *technological model*, sees the implementation of information systems and management science techniques causing a fundamental change in the governing process.[2] Problems and policy alternatives are now too complex for the public and its representatives to evaluate. Legislators solicit and follow the recommendations of professional administrators. The major source of power is information; the new norm of policy decision making is deference to expertise.[3]

Proponents of the technological model stress the importance of experts as the "new political actors."[4] However, in that portion of the political process

*Michael O. Boss died on December 21, 1975. We wish to dedicate this article to his children, Tanya, five, and Kari, three.

Authors' Note: The authors wish to acknowledge the support of the Research and Development Division, Center for Educational Policy and Management, during a portion of the time they devoted to the preparation of this paper. The Center for Educational Policy and Management is funded under a contract with the National Institute of Education, Department of Health, Education and Welfare. The research reported in this paper was conducted as part of the research and development of the center.

concerned with educational policy making, experts are certainly not new. Although historical interpretations may vary, there is consensus that educational experts, the superintendent and his professional staff, had become influential, if not dominant, actors by the 1920s.[5] The increase in political influence of experts in education predated similar developments in other arenas of decision making. As a result, a major thrust of the educational policy literature has been to emphasize the uniqueness of educational decision making. Research has been undertaken with the implicit assumption that education is more vulnerable to expert dominance than are other areas of public policy. Consequently, very few studies have been undertaken that compare decision making in school districts and other units of local government.[6] In view of the paucity of evidence, we agree with Paul E. Peterson, who offers the following admonition:

The literature on school politics may not be fundamentally incorrect in identifying a good deal of autonomy on the part of a small group of educational decision-makers. The central role that superintendents and their staff play in the decision-making process is well documented. . . . but the explanations and interpretations of this phenomenon depend heavily on the assumption that such influence relationships are peculiar to the field of education. Not only is such an assumption not demonstrated empirically, but it prevents scholars writing on the politics of education from seeing the broader implications of their field. . . . If decision-making patterns in education are the rule, not the exception, interpretations of American politics need to give greater weight to the role of experts, professionals and the directors of administrative structures than most political scientists generally have.[7]

Ironically, while other social scientists were recognizing the wider applicability of the technological decision-making model employed in the educational policy literature, some researchers were questioning the continued applicability of that model to educational policy making. The contention appeared in both popular and academic literature that the increasing politicization of education had changed the climate in which school officials must work to the extent that deference to expertise could no longer be the preponderant form of policy making.

On the surface, the turbulence of the 1960s certainly seemed to have contributed to politicization of education. Popular accounts of highly publicized conflicts portrayed professionals as struggling vainly against a variety of powerful interest groups. Professionals themselves were active in promulgating the view of the "beleaguered superintendent."[8] One observer quoted from the ranks of the beleaguered to support his contention that the world of the superintendent, as seen from the inside, is far more conflictual than the world as described by students of educational policy making:

The American school superintendent, long the benevolent ruler whose word was law, has become a harried, embattled figure of waning authority. . . . Brow beaten by once subservient boards of education, [teachers' associations], and parents, the superintendent can hardly be blamed if he feels he has lost control of his destiny. . . . Administrative powerlessness is becoming one of the most pervasive realities of organizational life.[9]

While some might be inclined to dismiss such testimony as self-serving, the view has been to some extent echoed by scholars who argue that the model of professional dominance is no longer correct. Representative of this argument is Donald J. McCarty and Charles E. Ramsey's *The School Managers*.[10] This study of 51 school districts in the Northeast and Midwest led them to conclude:

One can hardly avoid the view that today's educational administrator is engulfed in a pressure packed set of constraints. . . . Individuals previously without power are rapidly becoming aware of the strength that can be marshalled if they work together. . . . The tensions so apparent throughout American society have galvanized [school] boards into the political arena with a vengeance.[11]

The upshot of this controversy was a renewed interest in the question, "who governs school?" There was clearly a need for further research into relations among school boards, superintendents, and the public in order to test the hypothesis that patterns of influence were changing.[12] There was also a growing concern that educational policy researchers should make greater use of research techniques employed by other social scientists. Proponents of both the democratic and technological models of educational decision making had relied almost exclusively on the case-study approach. Their studies typically examined a small, unrepresentative sample of school districts and focused on major decisions in those districts. Consequently, they were not replicable, and their findings could not be generalized. A study based on a national sample of school districts systematically selected, which took a comprehensive view of the decision-making process, was a desirable complement to the growing literature subsumed under the rubric "politics of education."

The senior author undertook such a project in 1968 and published a portion of the results in 1974.[13] The focus of the study was on the school board, with lesser attention to the superintendent. Our focus in this paper is the reverse: The superintendent is the object of our analysis, with only modest attention to the school board.

At first glance, such a focus may seem inappropriate. However, most decisions are of course made by the superintendent with the concurrence of the school board. Our central focus on the superintendent is thus quite realistic. However, to concentrate on the interactions between interest groups and the superintendent raises the problem of professionalism as a legitimate concept.

If superintendents are experts, part of their authority rests in being "above politics." If, on the other hand, they are only decision makers, such a stance may prove impossible to maintain. Put another way, the aura of expertise may not survive in a decision-making arena freighted with interest group activity. Although political conflict may be generally discomforting, it is particularly discomforting in educational policy making.

"Children are precious creatures not to be subject to the vagaries of conflict." Thus argued the reformers of the early twentieth century and thus argue the administrators of today. Similarly, the general public has apparently readily accepted the legal independence of schools to ensure their separation from "conventional politics" and the associated group conflict.

So pervasive is this belief that the contest of an educational dispute is frequently of less concern to a community than the threat of conflict that accompanies the resolution of a dispute. Conflict avoidance is especially notable in school board elections. Aspiring candidates (at least those who are successful) avoid controversy and campaign on such platforms as "The best schools for the lowest cost." Whether conflict is in fact dysfunctional is not important. So long as conflict is perceived as threatening, *management* of conflict is a particularly valuable skill. It may be that conflict management is one of the more legitimate claims to expertise on the part of superintendents.

Management of conflict, if successful, increases the authority of the superintendent and reduces the influence of organized groups. Concurrent with the rise of technological society and its attendant reliance on experts, there has occurred a renewed demand for increased lay participation in governance. The resolution of the tensions is our essential task of conflict management.

Superintendents bring to this task some tangible resources that, if properly used, increase their influence over educational decisions. Most important, the superintendent is full time. He is able to devote his total energy and attention to matters within schools, whereas others, especially interest group leaders, are distracted by concern with family and occupation. Thus almost all routine decisions are resolved by the superintendent and his staff. Whereas each routine decision, taken individually, may be of no concern to interest groups, collectively such decisions constitute the great bulk of the business of the school district. The extent to which *all* decisions can be portrayed as routine strengthens the influence of the superintendent and diminishes access opportunities of interest groups.

Additionally, the routinization of decisions allows the superintendent to maximize another resource: a detailed knowledge of the organization and operation of the district unequaled by any group or individual in the community. It is a rare superintendent who cannot outmatch competition for influence, fact for fact, about budget, curriculum requirements, personnel standards, facilities, and legal requirements. School boards are frequently unable to acquire or distribute such information and hence prove to be of little help in mobilizing group support. Organizations that seek to achieve their goals by working with the school board find that they must circumvent the elected body to learn what they need to know. A substantial number of problems that arise within the school system increasingly appear to be highly technical in nature. Problems with reading programs thus take the form of complex analysis of achievement scores, reliability and validity measures, etc. Problems of budget and finance take the form of utilizing Planning, Programming, Budgeting System (PPBS) or similar comprehensive planning and budgetary methods. Problems of drawing school boundaries are expressed in terms of "mini-max" criteria utilized in linear programming. Interest groups, whatever the depth of their involvement in education, seldom have the skills necessary to understand problems cast in these very technical terms.

In contrast, the initial advantage of the superintendent is bolstered by staff assistance. As chief executive (albeit appointed), he can call on the full resources of the schools to assist him in the preparation of policy positions. An alternative source of information for interest groups, the school board, can do no more than rely on the superintendent. Most legislative and deliberative bodies have found it necessary to develop full-time, professional staff to try to break the bond of dependence on the executive. Proposals for comparable staff assistance by boards have met with resistance from superintendents for the obvious reason that independent staff for boards would create competing centers of expertise. Typical is the following excerpt from a management study commissioned by a large urban district:

The School Board members indicated some dissatisfaction with the quality of information provided to them by the District Administration. Although the Superintendent provides an extensive packet of information to the Board prior to each week's meeting, relating to significant events of the week, and providing supporting materials for items on the agenda, Board members feel they do not have all information necessary for making decisions. Two types of information appear to be missing from the Board's weekly packet: one is the continuous reporting of progress against plans and objectives; the other is the identification and evaluation of alternatives to actions recommended to the Board. As a result, Board members feel they are making decisions in many cases on the basis of inadequate information, and without any overall plan to provide a decision-making structure. Reflecting this concern, several Board members expressed a need for a Board staff with fiscal and information gathering skills. . . . This appears to be undesirable, since it could lead to an atmosphere of distrust and competition between the Board staff and the Administration.[14]

Such conclusions are based on a basic dogma of educational administration: *unity*. Robert H. Salisbury captures well the essence of the ideology:

Educators have tried very hard to achieve and maintain consensus among all those engaged in the educational enterprise. Unity is a prerequisite to a reputation for expertise, and it thus adds to the bargaining power of schoolmen as they seek public support. Unity inside the school helps justify independence from "politics."[15]

To the extent that organized interest groups seek to engage in influencing policy, then, they are handicapped by the ideology of unity. The administrative belief that educational decisions should be based on cool and reasoned judgments rather than political passions, when combined with the monopolizing of information, is a formidable barrier.

The barrier works both ways. Organized groups are denied legitimacy but also superintendents may find it difficult to deal effectively with organized groups that do achieve a sustained interest in educational policy. Their ideology prevents an easy acceptance of the "normal" pattern of bargaining, negotiation, and compromise.

The Problems of Conflict Management

We believe that the superintendent makes decisions in order to maximize a set of preferences based on his own values. It is in the interest of the superintendent, however, to minimize partisan response or community conflict regarding decision outcomes. All superintendents learn to live with some pressure and conflict, but all prefer to minimize them. The superintendent is thus constrained by the community (partially through interest groups) in making decisions and must further act to manage conflict that does arise.

We can specify three conditions that are necessary (and hence group activity) before decision-making conflict arises:

1. Decision outcomes are incongruent with community preferences.
2. Community mobilizes attempt to influence or constrain decision making.
3. Superintendent management of attempted influence is unsuccessful.

The first condition, incongruence of decision outcomes with community preferences, concerns the basic consensus of values between the community and the superintendents. If the superintendent and the community have similar value priorities and thus similar preferences, the superintendent is likely to make decisions that are satisfactory both to himself and to the community. Moreover, this occurs regardless of constraints. Indeed, there is little reason to attempt to constrain decision making by the superintendent. Obviously, this is an ideal case. Heterogeneity of values in the community precludes perfect congruence. The more that a decision outcome satisfies some preferences, the more it will inevitably dissatisfy other preferences. Further, nearly all superintendents place a greater priority on education than does the public at large. Superintendents would opt to carry on more activities at a higher cost than the community might find optimal. Finally, nearly all superintendents have a more universal view than the local community and are thus less likely to defer to more parochial local values. But the overall consensus of values between the superintendent and the community may be relatively high or relatively low. The greater the consensus, the greater the correspondence between decision outcomes and community preferences. The likelihood of attempts to influence or otherwise constrain is diminished. Conflict in decision making is likely to be low.

The second condition, community attempts to influence or constrain decision making, involves the problem of mobilizing for effecting political action. One fact of political life is that individuals in a community may be dissatisfied with a public decision but unable to do anything about it. Often action to oppose a decision is not worth the bother. Put in economic terms, the cost of acting is greater than the cost imposed by the decision. But even where action is clearly warranted, it may not be possible to organize properly to mount opposition to a decision. This is particularly the case for the schools, as they are insulated conventional political institutions. The more common mechanisms for political organization are simply not available. Political parties generally stay clear of local educational issues and politics. The myth that "politics should be kept out of the schools" effectively undermines the legitimacy of political organizations that seek to become involved in educational politics. Interest groups face a similar problem of legitimacy, and thus effectiveness, as organizational vehicles for influencing or constraining educational decisions. Interest groups appear to have marginal impact on educational policy making.

The dilemma is that it is apparently necessary to organize and mobilize across an entire community to effectively penetrate the educational decision-making system. This is obviously a difficult task. In larger communities, it may be a nearly impossible task. The single exception is crisis decision making. Then a different decision-making code is likely to prevail, one more akin to "normal" political processes. Such decisions are, however, in spite of the publicity attendant upon them, relatively scarce. In the normal cycle of a school year, probably not more than a fraction of decisions are nonroutine.[16]

The third condition, the management of attempted influence or reaction to decisions, reflects the action by superintendents in making and implementing decisions to minimize or to diffuse adverse response from the community. Conflict management does not involve tangible changes in decision outcomes but rather differences in decision-making style related to the articulation of issues, timing, and cultivation of support. Related to this is the development and maintenance of decision-making norms that isolate, render illegitimate, and undermine the effectiveness of potential opposition. Some forces are thus coopted into supporting a decision while others are completely excluded. The emphasis is on symbolic manipulation, an art of leadership that is learned and put to good use in decision making in order to reduce decision-making conflict.

Decision-making Conflict

We take as an indicator of the general level of decision-making conflict in a school district the superintendent's own assessment of such conflicts. The specific question asked whether there were any significant differences between the way the community views the superintendency and the way the superintendent, himself, views the superintendency.[17] Of the superintendents, 51 percent noted such differences. Some theorists would conceptualize the problem here in terms of role conflict. This approach is not incorrect, but our decision-making approach appears to be more theoretically and analytically fruitful. Moreover, open-ended replies to a second question probing the source of differences in views of the superintendency indicated in almost every case incongruent value priorities coupled with excessive decision-making constraints. This is precisely the kind of decision-making conflict that concerns us.[18]

Community Structure

Two facets of community structure interest us here, one pertaining to values and the other to political capability. High-status communities generally appear to give a higher priority to education than low-status communities do. This priority is reflected in higher levels of financial support, a greater scope of educational activity, greater community involvement in and support for school activities, and lower levels of decision-making conflict. The obvious reason is that the families that predominate in high-status communities generally owe their status to education. They work in professional, technical, and bureaucratic occupations that depend on education. Educators are included in these ranks. The consequence is a strong orientation to educational values in the community, a high consensus of values between educators and the community, and a basic deference to technical educational authority. Under such conditions, there is likely to be rather high general agreement about decision outcomes, a greater congruence between decisions and preferences, even in a low-constraint decision-making system. One key point here then is that there is less fundamental reason or need for group action to constrain educational decision-making in high-status communities than in low-status communities. Such action is likely to be supportive.

High-status communities generally are considerably more active in politics than are low-status communities. Participation in politics at the individual level is almost universally higher among the middle class. The breadth and intensity of interest group activity is almost universally higher in middle-class and upper-class communities. Such activity constitutes a major political resource greatly enhancing the capability of high-status communities to organize and mobilize to oppose, support, or otherwise constrain public decision-making. The means for exercising influence are already operative; it is a matter of directing such means towards the schools. The likely consequence is that high-status communities are potentially more active on a broader range of issues affecting the schools than low-status communities are.

There is a most fascinating paradox in our two conclusions here. We are arguing that high-status communities are likely to be prompt in reacting to educational policy but that the policy differences giving rise to negative reactions are rare. The demand for conflict management skills arises, of course, but management is likely to be effective or successful. In contrast, low-status communities are less apt to react to a policy, but when such reaction does occur, it is likely to be very intense and often nearly impossible for the superintendent to manage. The basic factors underlying decision-making conflict and the resultant group conflict in low-status communities and the high-status communities are thus qualitatively different.

Community Political Structure

The structure of community political action may be specific, general, or a mixture of both. Most local political action appears to be structured within the network of community voluntary groups and organizations. Pluralist theorists, notably David Truman and Robert Dahl, have repeatedly stressed the importance of interest groups to democratic (or responsive) policy making. Interest groups provide a ready mechanism for processing demands. The costs of organization has already been incurred, at least in part. Members of a particular group or organization are already partially sympathetic and sensitized to similar kinds of public concerns. Leadership has already been established. The resources of the entire group can be utilized, even if only a part of the group is actually aroused. Finally, the issue of concern may be rather narrow and specific. It is not necessary to involve the whole community but only those members of the group who share a particular concern. The advantages of utilizing existent interest groups to organize political action are so great that it is no surprise that political action is structured within the network of interest groups whenever possible.

The Group Structure of Educational Policy Making

One unresolved question in pluralist theory and in most empirical studies is whether political action organized through the existing interest group network can effectively influence or constrain public decision making. Our first task is to describe the areas of formal organizations that come to the attention of decision makers. We believe that there is an obvious bias in the mobilization of interests through the interest group network operative within the educational system (Table 2-1).

The Range of Group Activity

The different communication patterns of boards and superintendents are apparent. Not surprisingly, the most active group is the PTA, which can hardly be considered a source of potential conflict. PTAs tend to be supportive rather than demand articulating. They raise money for school activities not publicly funded, provide symbolic support for schools in bond referenda, and appear to be little more than an auxiliary organization to local administration, especially principals. Moreover, in the event they do shift from support to demand articulation, they tend to concentrate on narrow problems (usually associated with a specific school) rather than on districtwide policy.[19]

Beyond the PTA, group activity diminishes appreciably. It is somewhat surprising that PTAs so decidedly outrank teacher organizations, whose members have a more immediate interest in board policy. Given the growing militancy of teacher organizations, one should expect that they would be more active.

Table 2-1
Organizations Mentioned by Superintendents and Boards

Type of Interest Group	Superintendent ($N = 167$)	School Board Members ($N = 1139$)
PTA	57%	60%
Teachers	27%	31%
Left wing	24%	28%
Business-professional	35%	16%
Civil rights	24%	17%
Taxpayers	24%	16%
Right wing	25%	12%
League of Women Voters	18%	14%
Citizens' advisory committee	21%	13%
Religious	19%	11%
Service clubs	7%	20%
Neighborhood	7%	5%
Political	4%	5%
Labor	2%	3%

However, militancy is frequently exaggerated by the media. Although teacher organizations have achieved some influence over salary and working conditions, they have focused on these immediate problems and (with the notable exception of New York) have avoided efforts to influence more general policy.

In any case, boards and superintendents interact with PTAs and teacher organizations at about the same rate. Differences begin to appear when we examine organizations not directly or implicitly affiliated with the education "establishment." Most conspicuous are business and right-wing groups, who appear to seek out the superintendent twice as often as they do the school board. Citizens' advisory groups and religious groups also seem more interested in the superintendent than the board. Service clubs, in contrast (whose communications are likely to be supportive), concentrate on the board.

It appears then that despite the board's legal position as the elected representatives of the "public," that the superintendent is somewhat more likely to encounter potentially hostile groups. The ironies are apparent. According to traditional democratic theory and consistent with the ideology of educational administration, the superintendent as "expert" is to remain neutral. Although expert neutrality is a resource widely used by superintendents, they are also frequently called on to engage in "community relations." Certainly from the point of view of the public, superintendents are more visible than school boards. Thus a natural consequence of the superintendent's dominance of the board is his resultant role as the focus of group demands.

The response to such demands is another matter. Given the recruitment and occupational socialization of superintendents, we might expect that their reaction would be negative in that groups would appear to be "meddling." It is generally argued that superintendents prefer to narrow the focus of their communication to the "friends of education," when possible. Interaction with more contentious groups would therefore be behavior to be avoided by superintendents. To some extent, this notion is supported by the data. If we categorize organizations into two broad classifications, education related and non-education related, we gain some insight into the superintendent's response (Table 2-2).

Both board and superintendent agree that most attempts at influence come from the "outsiders." Only about one-fourth view educational organizations as involved in policy, compared to three-fourths who regard noneducation groups as so inclined. Our contention about the supportive nature of education groups is thus supported.

Much of the policy-influencing efforts of outside groups are viewed with hostility by both boards and superintendents. However, superintendents react more defensively than do boards. Such groups are believed to be critical of schools, opposed to financial measures, and critical of teachers. They are also regarded as less interested in schools than educational organizations. However, superintendents are more inclined toward such views than are boards. For

Table 2-2

Perception of Educational and Noneducational Organizations

	School Board	Superintendent
Interested in the Schools		
Education related[a]	62%	60%
Non-education related[b]	38%	40%
N[c]	542 (85%)	75 (70%)
Critical of Schools		
Education related	25%	2%
Non-education related	75%	98%
N	250 (39%)	40 (38%)
Support Financial Measures		
Education related	52%	61%
Non-education related	48%	39%
N	261 (41%)	62 (58%)
Oppose Financial Measures		
Education related	5%	4%
Non-education related	95%	96%
N	122 (19%)	25 (24%)
Attempt to Influence Education Program		
Education related	21%	25%
Non-education related	79%	75%
N	107 (17%)	36 (34%)
Critical of Teachers		
Education related	21%	0%
Non-education related	79%	100%
N	130 (20%)	32 (30%)
Would Defend Teachers		
Education related	46%	42%
Non-education related	54%	58%
N	332 (52%)	84 (79%)

[a]Education-related interest groups include PTA, citizen advisory groups, booster clubs, and similar groups.

[b]Non-education-related interest groups include all formal and informal groups or organizations aside from education-related interest groups.

[c]N is the number of respondents citing interest groups of some type in reply to open-ended questions. Multiple replies were coded in each case. Respondents citing no activity of particular type or citing individual or governmental entities are omitted.

example, 75 percent of the time that board members mentioned outside groups, they were regarded as critical of schools. Of the nominations by superintendents, 98 percent fell into this category.

Superintendents' views of specific organizations shed additional light on their communication with representatives of various publics (Table 2-3). The brunt of hostility from the outside comes from two groups of related ideology: taxpayers' groups and right-wing organizations, both of which are viewed with less alarm by boards. Surprisingly, their ostensible opponents, left-wing and civil rights groups, are viewed more benevolently. There is, then, a clear distinction being made, if outside participation is viewed with alarm, that some groups are more threatening than others. Superintendents are not, apparently, indiscriminately condemning all group participation. Rather, they are selective in their assessment.

Interest Groups and Decision Making

The problem we address now is what effect mobilized interest groups have on decision making. Our hypothesis is that if political action organized through interest groups is effective, then interest groups that are in opposition to particular educational decisions or critical of the pattern of decision making in general should be a source of decision-making conflict. Note that the concern here is with interest group *conflict*, groups that are explicitly identified as *dissatisfied* with educational policy.[20] Any impact of such interest group conflict on decision making should contribute to decision-making conflict. If interest group conflict does *not* result in decision-making conflict, this can be the case only if the impact of interest group conflict on decision making is trivial. The observed relationship between interest group conflict and decision-making conflict for our sample of school districts is given in Table 2-4.

Decision-making conflict is higher in those districts where interest group conflict is evident, in keeping with our hypothesis. The differences, however, are small. High interest group conflict appears to provide at best only a marginal increase (+9 percent) over the level of decision-making conflict expected when interest group conflict is not evident (51 percent). As an alternative view, consider that fully 40 percent of the cases of high interest group conflict fail to impact on decision making. The indications of interest group failure are much more impressive than the indications of success.

Interest groups act from a position of weakness due to their difficulty in gaining legitimacy within the educational realm. The dilemma is that most interest groups are viewed by the community and by decision-making authorities alike as having no fair claims within the schools. The "children's interests" should simply never yield to "special interests," especially "politically motivated

Table 2-3
Perception of Specific Organizations

Interest Groups	Most Interested		Supportive		Critical	
	Board Members	Superintendent	Board Members	Superintendent	Board Members	Superintendent
Educational						
PTA	48%	38%	15%	32%	5%	0%
Teachers	11	4	21	32	8	0
Citizens' advisory	6	7	6	5	1	1
Other educational	16	14	6	7	1	1
Community						
Service-civic	12	5	7	4	12	12
Business-professional	6	15	6	11	3	3
League of Women Voters	7	5	7	12	1	1
Neighborhood	3	1	0	0	1	6
Labor	1	1	2	4	2	4
Ideological						
Political	1	2	0	0	2	2
Left wing	0	0	16	23	3	6
Right wing	0	0	2	3	10	23
Taxpayers	0	0	1	1	15	22
Civil rights	5	7	6	5	10	10
Religious	2	0	2	11	4	4
Other Groups	3	2	7	14	3	4

Table 2-4
Decision-making Conflict and Community Political Structure

Community Political Structure		Decision-making Conflict	
		Low	High
Interest group conflict	Low	49%	51%
	High	40%	60%
			$N = 167$
General public conflict	Low	56%	44%
	High	28%	72%
			$N = 167$

interests." The principal advantage of interest groups in being able to organize around special needs thus also becomes their greatest liability.

The political processes in the larger community involves the frequent and continuous interaction of multiple issues. Interest groups operate in a political environment where opportunities for coalition formation and logrolling abound. The very heart of interest group theory centers on the means by which competing special interests coalesce and thereby determine decision outcomes. The political processes in the school system, however, more often involve single, isolated issues. The opportunities to form coalitions or to logroll are often nonexistent. Interest groups, rather than uniting, remain divided and powerless. Put another way, few single interest groups are sufficiently strong to stand by themselves, and few opportunities arise for interest groups to work together. The consequence is that the interest group network within the schools is doubly weak.

Many interest groups that attempt to influence decision making within the schools are so weak that superintendents ignore them for all meaningful purposes. Superintendents may listen to their demands politely, but the impact on decisions is minimal.[21] Most other interest groups are sufficiently weak that they are readily managed by the superintendent. Some are coopted. Most school districts, for example, have a host of committee posts waiting for interest group leaders. A surprising number of dissident interest group leaders become ardent supporters of the school through such processes. Other interest groups are isolated and played off, one against the other. Indeed, the shrewd superintendent ensures that every potentially threatening interest group is paired with an opposing interest group, even if the latter is a creation. Thus the only situation worse than an active John Birch Society and an active American Civil Liberties

Union (ACLU) is an active John Birch Society by itself. The key point in the management of interest group conflict is that few substantive changes in decisions are necessary. There is consequently a minimum of decision-making conflict.

The alternative to the interest group system is the general political mobilization of the community. Three major differences are evident between interest group conflict and general public conflict. First, general public conflict involves a very large part of the community, whereas interest group conflict usually involves only interest group leaders. There is thus a great discontinuity in the numbers of individuals involved. Second, general public conflict usually involves much more important issues than interest group conflict, at least in the eyes of the community. Major or critical issues are necessary in order to involve the entire community. Finally, general public conflict usually is much more episodic than interest group conflict. The interest group network persists over several issues. General public conflict more often rises and subsides with a single issue. In brief, general public conflict can be characterized as a political act of extreme magnitude but of short duration. Interest group conflict can be characterized as a political act of limited magnitude but of longer duration.

General public conflict is measured as follows:

1. *Intensity of organizational activity with respect to education.* Board members were asked eight open-ended questions in which they were to respond by listing the organized groups in the district that met the criteria of the questions. The maximum number of responses coded varied between two and three on each item. These questions concerned:

   a. Organizations most interested in the board.
   b. Organizations from which the board seeks support.
   c. Organizations working for passage of financial referenda.
   d. Organizations critical of the board.
   e. Organizations that attempt to influence teacher behavior in the classroom.
   f. Organizations that defend teachers when the latter are criticized.
   g. Organizations that attack teachers.

   The maximum possible number of specific organizations mentioned was 19. In constructing our organizational intensity measure, we calculated the mean number of groups mentioned by the members of each board. The resulting scores range from .20 to 11.14. The mean is 3.92, and the standard deviation is 2.74.

2. *General approval of board by groups within district.* The percentage of board members responding that no groups in the district were critical of the school

board was calculated for each board. The result was taken as our measure of group approval. Scores range from 1 to 98.1. The mean is 56, and the standard deviation is 3.497.

3. *Composite indicator of the level of educational problems.* The composite problem index ranges from 0 to 100. Its mean is 40.20, and its standard deviation is 23.10.

4. *Diversity of organizations active with respect to education.* (This summary measure was constructed from the same basic items on the board interview schedule as 1. above.) Each district was given one point for each type of group mentioned by board members in their responses to the eight open-ended questions. The resulting sum for each district was taken as an indicator of the diversity of educationally active organizations it contained. Scores range from 1 to 12. The mean is 6.57, and the standard deviation is 2.78.

5. *The level of consensus regarding education.* This is a straight percentage of the members of each board who replied negatively to the question: *"Is there any tension or conflict among people in the district on questions having to do with school policies?"* Scores range from 1 to 98. The mean is 45.08, and the standard deviation is 27.93.

6. *The extent to which groups contact the board.* This measure too was based on a single question and reflects the percentage of board members on each board who responded affirmatively to the question: *"Do any representatives of community groups or organizations ever contact you personally or seek your support for their position?"* Scores range from 1 to 98. The mean is 64.14, and the standard deviation is 25.19.

7. *Role consensus between the board and the public.* Board members were asked which of the following points of view best approximated the way they approach their jobs:

   a. The board member "should do what the public wants him to do even if it isn't his own personal preference."
   b. The board member "should use his own judgment regardless of what other want him to do."

They were also asked: *"How do you think the people of the district feel about the two points of view? Do you think they want you to follow their wishes even if you disagree with them or to use your own judgment?"* The percentage of members on each board who felt that their approach to the job was consistent with what the public wanted (regardless of which view that may have been) was taken as our indicator of role consensus. Scores range from 1 to 98. The mean is 52.74, and the standard deviation is 24.66.

8. *Popularity of board policy positions.* The proportion of the members of each board who indicated that they rarely or never did "take a stand that the majority of the public seems to disagree with" was computed. Scores on this variable run from 1 to 98. Its mean is 64, and the standard deviation is 25.19.

These eight variables and their respective factor loadings are listed in Table 2-5.

The immediate impact of general public conflict on decision making is likely to be limited in time. Our concern here is with the long-term or aftereffects of general public conflict. General public conflict so severely strains conflict management capabilities that decision-making authorities are likely to become hypersensitive to further outbursts. Such sensitivity will be evidenced in heightened perceptions of decision-making conflict in general. Looking again at Table 2-4, such a pattern is evident. Decision-making conflict is significantly higher in school districts where general public conflict has been in evidence than in school districts where general public conflict has not been experienced. Nearly three-quarters of the superintendents who have experienced general public conflict also experience decision-making conflict. As a matter of comparison, general public conflict has twice the impact of interest group conflict even though it is less frequent and of limited duration.

The management of general public conflict is an entirely different problem from the management of interest group conflict. Interest group conflict is limited to bargaining between the superintendent and interest group leaders, many of whom are friends of the superintendent. Many opportunities for negotiated settlement arise should the tactics of cooptation or isolation fail.

Table 2-5
Variables Significantly Loaded on the Tension Factor

Variable	Factor Loading
Intensity of organizational activity with respect to education	.76307
General approval of board by groups within district	−.88936
Composite indicator of the level of educational problems	.78065
Diversity of organizations active with respect to education	.76307
The level of consensus regarding education	−.75550
The extent to which groups contact the board	.73116
Role consensus between the board and the public	−.52817
Popularity of board policy positions	−.49135

General public conflict is more apt to be a mass movement. The latter are most easily managed through symbolic manipulation. Symbolic rewards serve to diffuse the movement with minimum impact upon the substance of decisions. The superintendent, however, has a very limited capability to distribute symbolic rewards. More often the school board monopolizes what is essentially the legitimation function in cases of general public conflict. The principal resources of the superintendent, professional reputation and expertise, have small value once general public conflict becomes heated. The key point is that the superintendent has such limited ability to manage general public conflict that such conflict is likely to be evident as a source of decision-making conflict.

Superintendent Professionalism

The professional superintendent is at once an ideologue and a practitioner. He combines a commitment to an ideal set of educational values with the political skills necessary to obtain these values. The professional ideology of the superintendent may prove to be a source of decision-making conflict with the local community. The local community will always give priority to a broader set of values than the superintendent. The stronger the ideological commitment of the superintendent, the greater the potential for decision-making conflict. Actual practice dictates ideological compromise. Value demands are relaxed to the level of political skill in managing decision-making conflict. Simultaneously, however, political skills increase with practice. Superintendents are able to maximize their educational values according to the level of their political skill.

There is an important qualification here. Superintendents may not choose to expend their total political resources. The marginal gain in values may not warrant such expenditure. Some superintendents may choose to act at the limits of their capability to gain maximum values. Other superintendents may choose to act at a more relaxed level to gain satisfactory, but not maximum values. The latter case reduces the likelihood of decision-making conflict. Our assumption is that the most professional superintendents are value maximizers. They operate at the limit of their political skills under conditions of greater decision-making conflict.

Two propositions relating superintendent professionalism to decision-making conflict are of particular concern here. First, we expect that superintendents with the doctorate degree would experience decision-making conflict more often than superintendents with the masters degree. Individuals who complete the doctoral program in education or educational administration tend to be ideologues. The reason is quite simple: Only an ideologue has the commitment to complete such programs.

Second, we expect that superintendents with experience gained either in the present position (tenure) or in another position (previous experience) would experience decision-making conflict less frequently than superintendents without experience. Superintendents with experience either relax their ideological commitment or gain the political skills to effect their value priorities or employ some combination of both. We suspect that the last is the case.

To test our propositions, the incidence of decision-making conflict among superintendents with differing degree rank, experience, and tenure was examined. The findings are given in Table 2-6. The pattern of decision-making conflict conforms to the attributes of superintendent professionalism as hypothesized. Superintendents with the doctorate degree show a higher incidence of decision-making conflict than superintendents with the master's degree. Superintendents with experience or tenure show a lower incidence of decision-making conflict than superintendents without experience or tenure. The measured differences here appear small. True differences are likely to be greater than the measured differences, however. Degree rank and experience are confounded and the effect of one tends to undercut the apparent effect of the other.

The true effects of degree rank and experience upon the incidence of decision-making conflict are better indicated by a hierarchical model that includes both independent variables at one time, as reported in Table 2-7. Superintendents with no previous experience and low tenure are ranked low. Superintendents with either previous experience or high tenure are ranked high. The apparent mediating effects of experience on decision-making conflict continue to hold. The crucial finding is that inexperienced doctorates are subject to a significantly higher incidence of decision-making conflict than any other group of superintendents. This is precisely in keeping with our theoretical

Table 2-6
Superintendent Professionalism and Decision-making Conflict

Superintendent Characteristic		Decision-making Conflict	
		Low	High
Degree rank	Low	49%	51%
	High	35%	65%
			$N = 167$
Experience	Low	35%	65%
	High	54%	46%
			$N = 104$
Tenure	Low	39%	61%
	High	49%	51%
			$N = 167$

Table 2-7
High Decision-making Conflict and Degree Rank-Experience-Tenure Interaction

		Degree Rank	
		Low	High
Experience and tenure	Low	58%[a]	86%
		(19)	(15)
	High	49%	51%
		(48)	(22)
		$N = 167$	

[a]Figure given is percentage of cases with high decision-making conflict evident. Figure in parentheses is cell N.

expectations. Inexperienced doctorates are likely to have the highest level of ideological zeal, the fundamental source of decision-making conflict, and the lowest level of political skill necessary to manage such conflict.

Professionalism and Conflict Management

We have examined some effects of community political structure and superintendent professionalism on decision-making conflict. General public conflict and to a lesser degree interest group conflict as well as professional ideology appear to be sources of decision-making conflict. Professional experience appears to increase the conflict management skills of the superintendent and thus reduce decision-making conflict. We now treat superintendent professionalism and community political structure together in order to examine in greater detail the effects of superintendent professionalism on conflict management.

We begin with the assumption that if general public conflict and interest group conflict are not managed, decision-making conflict is likely to result. Community political action is not always successful in mobilizing and reaching its target. The relationship is thus not always perfect, but it is high. We can further assume then that the effect of conflict management is to reduce this relationship. General public conflict or interest group conflict will be evident, but decision-making conflict does not arise. Our analytic strategy then is to look at cases of high general public conflict and high interest group conflict and to examine the effects of superintendent professionalism on increasing or mitigating the observed decision-making conflict. We expect the incidence of decision-making conflict to be higher where ideology is strong because the underlying value tensions are greater and thus conflict management is likely to be a more difficult problem. Conversely, we expect the incidence of decision-making conflict to be lower where experience is high because conflict management skills are greater. The results of our analysis are reported in Table 2-8.

Our findings strongly support our theoretical expectations. Superintendents with the doctorate degree appear to experience considerably more difficulty in managing both general public conflict and interest group conflict than superintendents with the master's degree do. The incidence of decision-making conflict that results from community-based conflict is 20 to 30 percent higher for doctors than for masters. Doctors do have less experience on the whole than masters. This accounts for part of the difference but is insufficient to account for the entire difference. Our conclusion must be that conflict management is a more fundamentally difficult problem where ideology, a characteristic of the doctorate group, is strong.

Superintendents with experience, whether gained through tenure in the present position or experience in a previous position, appear to experience much greater success in managing both general public conflict and interest group conflict than superintendents without experience of any kind. The incidence of decision-making conflict that results from community-based conflict is 20 to 30 percent lower for the high-experience and high-tenure groups. Note that apparent success in managing conflict is greater in the case of interest group conflict than in the case of general public conflict. The percentage reduction in the incidence of decision-making due to interest group conflict is nearly double that due to general public conflict. We suggested earlier that the management of interest group conflict was an easier problem than the management of general public conflict. The findings here support that contention. Through experience, the superintendent learns to deal readily and effectively with interest group conflict, and it rapidly diminishes as a source of decision-making conflict. In

Table 2-8
Decision-making Conflict and Superintendent-School District Interaction

Superintendent Characteristic		School District	
		High Public Conflict	High Interest Group Conflict
Degree rank	Master's	61%[a]	48%
	Doctorate	88%	80%
Experience	Low	83%	73%
	High	64%	42%
Tenure	Low	80%	76%
	High	62%	42%

[a]Figure given is percentage of cases with high decision-making conflict evident.

essence, interest groups are, compared to other arenas of policy making, trivial in education. Even with regard to the widely publicized occasions of involuntary turnover among superintendents, interest groups appear to be less responsible than is commonly believed. Compared to loss of general public confidence, interest group activity is unrelated to superintendent turnover.[22]

It appears that an additional component of expertise, successful conflict management, is poorly served by a high degree of professional commitment and well served by a strong dose of on-the-job training.

Comments

Fred G. Burke

Introduction

Boss et al, present a detailed analysis of the complex relationships among school superintendents, their communities, and interest groups. Consideration of the interaction between interest groups and school superintendents, which the authors state in the opening paragraph to be their sole concern, occupies a small part of their paper. The bulk of their attention is devoted to an examination of local school decision making, which to their minds depends on the professional background of local superintendents, the socioeconomic makeup of local communities, and the degree of congruity between the value preferences of the superintendents and local communities. In their view, interest groups have little effect on educational policy decisions. Interest group conflict seldom leads to what the authors term "decision-making conflict," which is assumed to be a significant indicator of interest group success in affecting policy matters in local school districts.

They also contend that the capacity of local school superintendents to effectively "manage" conflicts depends on the degree to which the superintendents are either ideologues or experienced. The more educational credentials superintendents possess, the more ideological superintendents are, and the more conflicts they incur. The presumption is that if superintendents were good at managing conflicts, there would be fewer of them. Likewise, the authors argue that the more experienced superintendents are, the fewer conflicts they face. Less successful conflict managers are those superintendents who are both inexperienced and highly credentialed.

In my review of the article, I will examine several key assumptions regarding the importance of congruity in value preferences between superintendents and their respective communities. I also want to challenge the authors' claim that schools are, as they put it, "insulated conventional political institutions." I will argue to the contrary and suggest further that this judgment on the authors' part reflects a general naïveté toward the everyday realities of school life that significantly undercuts their analysis. Third, I will suggest that the authors' hypothesis that relates the professional characteristics of superintendents to their skills in managing decision-making conflicts confuses ideology with credentials. And by relying on the widely acknowledged notion that superintendents acquire management skills on the job, the authors shed little new light on the problem under investigation.

In my conclusion, I will propose an alternative view that attempts to accommodate some of the considerations raised by the paper under discussion.

Community and Superintendent Value Preferences

At the outset, I question whether the authors have pinpointed an important component in the decision-making process when they examine divergences in values between communities and superintendents. The authors report that 51 percent of the superintendents studied did note such differences. On the other hand, it is evident that 49 percent of the superintendents did not perceive any separation between the community's view of their job and their own. Is there anything significant revealed here?

Aside from the question of relevance, I would like to raise two concerns. First, a question regarding theory. Do differences of opinion on the role of superintendents constitute differences in values? If so, do differences preclude congruence? It is conceivable to me that given the way in which the question was asked, superintendents could have a set of highly professional and technical values that their communities do not share. But that fact in and of itself does not mean that the values are necessarily incongruent. It could be inferred that the value priorities of superintendents may simply be a means for achieving the value priorities of the community. In other instances, the respondents may well hold different values than their communities, but they may also have decided to submerge these values for the purposes of survival, advancement, or success in achieving other shared educational goals. This seemingly semantic problem points to the difficulties inherent in "value analysis."

Second, I find the characterizations of both superintendents and particular communities at variance with the facts as I know them. The authors claim that superintendents are likely to have a "more universal view," and to place a higher priority on education. In contrast, communities are imputed to have more parochial concerns at hand. High-status communities, it is asserted, assign a higher priority to education, provide better financial and moral support for their schools, and are less likely to experience a great deal of decision-making conflict. Low-status communities seldom react to educational policies, and when they do, the reaction is described by the authors to be "intense" and "nearly impossible" for the conflict manager to handle.

I would question whether superintendents have a "more universal" view than their communities. In some instances, boards of education choose superintendents who share their parochial view of the world. In others, particularly professional communities, the residents are far more "universal" in their outlook than their employee. This is due in large measure to the fact that superintendents are often the products of provincial teacher colleges and a hide-bound certification process.

I take strong exception to the authors' depiction of educational values by community type. For example, if one were to balance local education costs against a community's ability to pay, it is clear that low-income and lower-middle-income communities make a much greater effort to support public education than wealthier communities. Also I find residents in high-status communities are much more critical about the education their children receive. They themselves are highly schooled and show little deference to educational professionals. Incidences of conflict are generally high in these school communities.

However, I find it difficult in sum to relate incidences of school conflict to community types. While one can argue, as I have above, that high-status communities experience a great deal of decision-making conflict in education, it appears just as easy to me to suggest that low-working and lower-middle-class communities experience a proportionate share of conflicts too. Northern city desegregation controversies serve as good examples. In many ways, one could even claim that working- and lower-middle-class communities have a more sophisticated network of neighborhood ethnic and political organizations with which to apply pressure on educational decision makers. Hence, insofar as education is concerned, it seems inappropriate for many reasons to assert that incidences of decision-making conflict are related to status or to attribute a priori particular values to particular status groups.

Schools as Political Institutions

The authors err when they refer to schools as "insulated conventional political institutions," and this misconception undermines their thesis that interest groups have a minimal impact on educational decision making.

First, I would argue that schools are the least insulated of our public institutions. I know of no other delivery system for public services that casts as wide a net in terms of participation or that has as many entry points for citizen pressure as do schools. Traditionally, both policy-making authority and the financial burden for supporting education has been vested in local jurisdictions. Though states have assumed a more direct share of the cost and authority for educational policy in the past decade, public schools have retained their uniquely local character and have remained remarkably open—some would say vulnerable—public institutions.

However, the old nostrum that "politics should be kept out of the schools" is indeed a myth, as the authors suggest. Conventional politics does intrude on local school governance in fairly straightforward, conventional ways. School board posts are often stepping-stones for political aspirants. If one examines carefully the way in which school contracts are awarded for transportation, materials, and food, or if one were privy to the input on nonprofessional personnel decisions (i.e., clerical, cafeteria, and school safety workers), one would find the normal political process hard at work. And supposing that a fraction of the complaints of teacher organizations proved accurate, then it would appear that political influence, not merit, is a prime determinant in promotion, particularly in big-city systems.

Interest groups, aside from partisan political activities, constitute a potent force in the educational decision-making process. However, it appears that the authors' research design is inadequate to make such a judgment. For example, I find it extraordinary that only 27 percent of the superintendents sampled listed teachers' organizations as active interest groups. This figure seems so low an indicator of teacher organization activity that it casts doubt in my mind as to the representativeness of the authors' sample.

Another problem is that the effect of interests groups is measured by assessing their impact in *opposing* educational policy decision and then only indirectly by sifting their impact through conflict levels that are never distinguished in a discernible manner. Thus it is not clear at all that the "decision-making" conflict discrepancies between districts with a high and low "interest group" conflict is significant by any measure.

But the authors' perception of interest groups and their mode of operating proves most troublesome to this writer. They speculate—far beyond the reach of their data—that interest groups fail to have an impact on educational decisions because they are unable to obtain standing in educational decision-making realms. They argue that since school politics often revolve around single, isolated issues, it is difficult for interest groups to engage in logrolling and other coalition-building activities. The result is that interest groups "remain divided and powerless."

For my part, I find little evidence in the field to support this view. First, it is apparent to me that interest groups have been quite effective in shaping educational policy, as any quick culling of national controversies surrounding desegregation, textbook choice, and the basic skills would indicate. Second, interest groups are arising increasingly as organizational responses to particular issues. They emerge, coalesce with other one-issue interest groups, register their effect, and subside. The fact that they organize around special needs improves, not detracts from, their effectiveness. For example, a citizens' group that mobilizes against forced busing can be highly effective because it can target its resources and maximize its energies over a short period of time. It can generate all its emotion in a short burst precisely because it has no institutional future at stake. Third, I would suggest Oliver Garceau's notion of interest groups as shifting constellations in a continuing political process to be more appropriate for understanding the politics of public schools than the more synchronic formulations of David Truman and Robert Dahl.

Conflict Management and the Characteristics of Superintendents

I share the view expressed by the authors that experience improves the skills of superintendents in handling conflict situations. The reasons are self-evident and need no further comment. But the authors also find that more highly schooled superintendents do not manage conflicts as well as their less-learned brethren. They conclude ipso facto that the well-educated superintendents must be ideologues. The authors have no data to support this claim. Further, it appears to me that they are confusing credentials with conviction.

It is a truism that higher-education degrees are fast becoming prerequisites for all sorts of positions in our public institutions. Schools, as our society's credential vendors, have always had a stake in building course requirements and degrees into job specifications. Our advancement in our public school systems has depended on the aquisition of more courses, degrees, and certificates. I find it hard to believe that any content acquired by professional educators in continued classwork superseded their basic motivation that is usually to satisfy the institutional imperative. Though I can offer no alternative explanation for the discrepancy the authors have disclosed, I find their notion unconvincing.

An Alternative View

I would like to suggest an alternative framework as a starting point for further analysis. Such a framework, or perspective, for understanding some of the contemporary facets of local school governance would need to take into account some fundamental shifts occurring in local educational policy making.

It is clear that states are assuming more authority for assuring an equal educational opportunity for all children. A change of this magnitude of necessity will affect local policy-making bodies and educational professionals. Public school policy decisions, once developed largely in a local vacuum, will need to be coordinated and rationalized with directions set by the state. When specific state mandates (e.g., school desegregation) have been enforced in the past, the effects have sometimes been unsettling for local communities. As states, through a variety of accountability statutes, assert more oversight responsibilities, its impact on local decision making will be increasingly felt.

I sense also that local decision-making rules are changing. The relative unanimity depicted by the authors between superintendents and school boards appears to be diminishing. School boards are demanding a larger role in the everyday matters of educational administration. I know of many examples where school superintendents experience as much, if not more, conflict with the school boards that appointed them as they do with the public at large. The rhetoric of greater participation in the sixties is shaping educational decision making in the seventies.

An unforeseen effect of the increased state role in educational affairs is that the structure and ideology of interest groups begins to reflect the changes in educational governance. Local affiliates of school administrators' groups, school boards' associations, and teacher organizations start reflecting extralocal concerns and policy positions. State organizations in turn attempt to better coordinate interest group activities of the various local communities. State interest group representatives also strive to influence educational policy decisions at the top with the knowledge that state-level action may pay dividends for their clients in local communities.

But perhaps the most significant factor on which future directions in educational decision-making will depend is the rapidly evolving nature of our political culture. We are entering an era of participatory consensus. Contemporary organizations, particularly those involved with public education, must provide for the broadest involvement of the public if they are to achieve the purpose for which they were originally designed. Authoritarian hierarchy, as an organizational style, must rapidly give way to new, diffuse, and as yet ill-defined forms characterized by wide participation and consensus building.

There is little precedent to guide these new processes. Considerable opposition from within organizations and from the external power structure is rampant. The temptation to escape the tedious uncertainty of consensus building and to plan *for* people rather than with them is difficult to resist.

Nevertheless, the rapidity of change in a postindustrial society will necessitate both a willingness and an increased tolerance for constantly altered forms of organization. Organizational commitment must be obtained through means other than traditional, institutionalized means, placing greater emphasis on its purposes and goals, and less on the organization as a means to personal security. Since the changing purposes of organization will tend to create a host of unanticipated consequences, rapid feedback mechanisms and simulations of alternative futures must be designed.

Edmund Burke has said that "you can never plan the future by the past." This seems to be an accurate depiction of the kind of world in which public education will find itself over the next quarter century. As our political culture changes, so must educators and the schools.

Notes

1. See, for example, Robert L. Heilbroner, *An Inquiry into the Human Prospect* (New York: W.W. Norton, 1974); and Victor L. Ferkiss, *The Future of Technological Civilization* (New York: George Braziller, 1974).

2. The contradiction between concurrent demands for direct control of leaders on the one hand and for increasing government initiative on policy development on the other is well noted in Henry Jacoby, *The Bureaucratization of the World* (Berkeley: University of California Press, 1973).

3. Don K. Price, "Knowledge and Power," in *Science and Policy Issues*, ed. Paul J. Piccard (Itasca, Ill.: F.E. Peacock, 1969). See also Guy Benveniste, *The Politics of Expertise* (Berkeley, Calif.: Glendessary Press, 1972).

4. Allan W. Lerner, *Experts, Politicians, and Decisionmaking in the Technological Society* (General Learning Press, forthcoming).

5. David Tyack, *The One Best System* (Cambridge, Mass.: Harvard University Press, 1974), pp. 126-176. See also James W. Guthrie et al., "The Erosion of Lay Control," in National Commission for Citizens in Education, *Public Testimony on Public Schools* (Berkeley, Calif.: McCutchan Publishing, 1975), pp. 92-101.

6. R.J. Snow, *Local Experts: Their Roles as Conflict Managers in Municipal and Educational Government* (Ph.D. dissertation, Northwestern University, 1966), and Roland L. Warren et al., *The Structure of Urban Reform* (Lexington, Mass.: D.C. Heath, 1974) are examples of such efforts.

7. Paul E. Peterson, "The Politics of American Education," in *Review of Research in Education*, ed. Fred N. Kerlinger (Itasca, Ill.: F.E. Peacock, 1974), p. 365.

8. This apt phrase is found in William Boyd, "The Public, The Professionals, and Educational Policy-Making: Who Governs?" (Paper presented at the American Educational Research Association Annual Meeting, Washington, D.C., 1975), p. 7.

9. Gene I. Maeroff, "Harried School Leaders See Their Role Waning," *New York Times*, March 5, 1974, pp. 1, 29, © 1974 by the New York Times Company. Reprinted with permission; Donald A. Erickson, "Moral Dilemmas of Administrative Powerlessness," *Administrators' Notebook*, April 1972, pp. 3-4, cited in Boyd, "The Public, The Professionals, and Educational Policy-Making," p. 8.

10. Donald J. McCarty and Charles E. Ramsey, *The School Managers* (Westport, Conn.: Greenwood Publishing, 1971).

11. Ibid., pp. 53-211, 213.

12. It should be noted that most of the proponents of the beleaguered suprintendent position viewed threats to expertise as originating from outside

the local community (court decisions, administrative regulations, etc.), or from the increasing organizational efforts of teachers.

13. L. Harmon Zeigler and M. Kent Jennings with G. Wagner Peak, *Governing American Schools* (North Scituate, Mass.: Duxbury Press, 1974).

14. Seattle School District, *Management-Organization Study* (December 1975).

15. Robert H. Salisbury, "Schools and Politics in the Big City," *Harvard Educational Review* 38 (1967): 417. Reprinted with permission.

16. Our current examination of roll call votes in 11 school districts indicates that approximately 95 percent of the recorded votes are unanimous.

17. The sample is described in L. Harmon Zeigler and M. Kent Jennings, with G. Wagner Peak, *Governing American Schools* (North Scituate, Mass.: Duxbury Press, 1974) pp. 256-261.

18. The question: "Are there any important differences between what you think the job of superintendent involves and the way the public sees it? Just what are these differences?"

19. Frederick M. Wirt and Michael W. Kirst, *The Political Web of American Schools* (Boston: Little, Brown, 1972), pp. 53-55.

20. In *Governing American Schools*, our measure was of group *intensity*. See Zeigler and Jennings, with Peak, *Governing American Schools*, pp. 98-99. In this essay, we use the same measurement technique but apply it only to that subset of the groups indicating some degree of dissatisfaction: (1) organizations most interested in education, (2) organizations working for defeat of financial referenda, (3) organizations critical of schools, (4) organizations attempting to influence the educational program, and (5) organizations critical of teachers.

21. L. Harmon Zeigler and Michael O. Boss, "Pressure Groups and Public Policy: The Case of Education," in *The Policy Vacuum*, ed. Robert N. Spadaro et al., (Lexington, Mass.: Lexington Books, 1975). In addition, our examination of 11 school districts indicates that of the total communications received by a superintendent in board meetings, cabinet meetings, or in informal interaction, less than 3 percent is generated by interest groups other than the PTA.

22. The partial correlation between organizational activity and superintendent turnover is $-.07$, controlling for decline of mass support and metropolitanism. See Zeigler and Jennings, with Peak, *Governing American Schools*, p. 111.

3

Political Perspectives on Recent Efforts to Reform School Finance

Donna E. Shalala and
Mary Frase Williams

The effort to change the way in which public schools are financed is part of a larger debate about American federalism that has been going on since pre-Revolutionary War days. Looking at recent activities in the field of school finance provides another arena in which to examine the forces contributing to the greater centralization of the American system of government.

For now the issue of what level of government will bear primary responsibility for financing education has been resolved in favor of the states. The conclusion is noteworthy since decentralization, under the label "local control," has always been the watchword of American public education. Interestingly, while centralization has taken place at the federal level in many fields, on this issue it has occurred at the level of state government.

School finance has been one of the educational issues most discussed in the past five years. While there are issues in school finance that are pertinent primarily at the local level (e.g., contract negotiations and the increasing defeats of school measures in local tax and bond elections), this article will focus on the movement in the 1970s to change the means of financing public education within individual states.

It also discusses the process of change and the conditions that facilitate and impede change. In the first part of the decade, a number of states implemented new school finance systems, and it appeared more would do so in subsequent years. However, other states failed to adopt new systems in the early seventies, and more recently the movement for change has slowed considerably. An examination of the politics of school finance reform reveals several factors that explain these patterns and that may be applicable to other issues.

Background

Financing public elementary and secondary education involves all three levels of government, but the relative roles of each level have changed over time. State involvement in local schools was minimal in the early days of the republic, but it began to grow in the second half of the nineteenth century.[1] However, the states' role in financing public education was still relatively minor in the first three decades of the twentieth century as can be seen from Table 3-1. Under that decentralized system of school finance, most school revenues came from the local property tax.

One result of such a system was great differences in the level of school expenditures between districts within the same state. Districts with strong property tax bases could provide high levels of expenditures, and those with little taxable property could not. Reformers became concerned with the inequity of such a system in the 1920s and 1930s. Their efforts led to the development of new formulas for the distribution of state aid for education to local school districts. One element in these formulas was an equalization provision that linked the amount of aid a school system would receive to its ability to finance education from local resources. Under such provisions property-poor school districts received more aid per pupil than districts with stronger tax bases.

The institution of equalization-aid programs led to less reliance on locally raised revenues to finance education and to an increase in the proportion of funds provided by the state government. This development is reflected in the substantial rise in the state's role in school finance between 1929-30 and 1939-40. The state share increased again in the next decade, but between 1950 and 1970 there was little change except for the increase in the role of the federal government with the passage of the Elementary and Secondary Education Act in 1965.

Beginning in the late 1960s, some educators, scholars, and reformers again turned their attention to the manner in which public schools were financed. The major proportion of school monies still comes from the local property tax. The only other substantial contributor is state government. In 1974-75 the National Education Association (NEA) estimated that approximately 49 percent of education monies was provided locally, 44 percent was provided by the states, and 8 percent was provided by the federal government. Contributions, of course, vary considerably from state to state. In 1974-75, for example, Hawaii's

Table 3-1

Sources of Revenue for Public Elementary and Secondary Schools in Selected Years (1919 to 1969)

School Year	Federal Government (%)	State Governments (%)	Local Districts (%)
1919-20	0.3	16.5	83.2
1929-30	0.4	16.9	82.7
1939-40	1.8	30.3	68.0
1949-50	2.9	39.8	57.3
1959-60	4.4	39.1	56.5
1969-70	8.0	39.9	52.1

Source: National Center for Educational Statistics, Department of Health, Education and Welfare, *Digest of Education Statistics, 1972 Edition* (Washington, D.C.: Government Printing Office, 1973), p. 68.

state government provided 89 percent of the revenues for the state's public schools while the New Hampshire state government contributed only 7 percent.[2]

The activities of the last ten years have not focused on expenditure disparities between states, although this was a major issue throughout the history of the federal debate on general aid to education. Rather, the concern has been with variations in school expenditures among school districts within a state.

In almost every state some districts provide two to three times the level of educational resources per pupil as other districts. Further research suggested that a major cause of such differences was the uneven distribution of property wealth per pupil among school districts. Districts low in property wealth would frequently tax themselves at higher-than-average rates, yet realize less-than-average expenditure levels. Ironically, districts with strong tax bases frequently spent higher-than-average sums on education while being able to maintain lower-than-average tax rates. Thus school expenditures varied directly with the property wealth of a local school district rather than with the tax effort a community exerted to finance public education.

It was this relationship between local property wealth and school expenditures that troubled the new generation of school finance reformers. In the search for additional funds and more equitable financing schemes, they have turned their attention to both federal and state governments.

The Federal Arena

The states won the debate about what level of government should have greater influence over the resources available and the equity of distribution schemes for public education only after efforts to get the federal government to play a major role in this area failed. After ten years of activity in Washington, school finance reformers went back to their state capitals. The return to the states reflected the unwillingness of the federal government to provide adequate redress for the inequities that motivated the reformers. Three pieces of evidence lead to this conclusion. Each concerns a different federal institution.

1. *The failure to increase the federal role in financing public schools.* When the Elementary and Secondary Education Act of 1965 (ESEA) was passed, there was a substantial hope that the federal role in financing education would continue to expand, substituting revenues raised by the progressive national income tax for revenues derived from the regressive local property tax. This has not occurred. Federal aid represents no more of the total revenues for education in 1974-75 than it did in the first year of ESEA (see Table 3-2).

A second hope was that the package of programs in ESEA—particularly Title I, the program targeted at poor children—would reduce differences in the resources available for rich and poor school districts. Title I has had such an equalizing effect, putting more resources in areas with larger numbers of poor

Table 3-2

Revenue Received from Federal, State, and Local Sources for Public Elementary and Secondary Schools

School Year	Federal Sources (%)	State Sources (%)	Local Sources (%)
1960-61	3.8	39.8	56.4
1961-62	4.3	38.7	56.9
1962-63	3.6	39.3	57.1
1963-64	4.4	39.3	56.4
1964-65	3.8	39.7	56.5
1965-66	7.9	39.1	53.0
1966-67	7.9	39.1	53.0
1967-68	8.0	39.3	52.7
1968-69	7.4	40.0	52.6
1969-70[a]	7.2	40.9	51.8
1970-71	8.4	39.4	52.1
1971-72	8.9	38.3	52.8
1972-73	7.9	40.6	51.5
1973-74	8.2	42.6	49.2
1974-75	7.8	43.6	48.6

[a]The slight differences for 1969-70 between Tables 3-1 and 3-2 are the result of different methods for computing these statistics on the part of the NEA and the National Center for Educational Statistics.

Source: National Education Association, *Estimates of School Statistics, 1974-75*, p. 16.

children. However, the other ESEA titles and additional federal programs have not necessarily directed the greatest aid to needy pupils or districts.[3] Thus the overall federal impact has not had the equalizing effect many had envisioned.

While some congressmen have been concerned with this issue, Congress has not passed legislation that would actively involve the federal government in school finance reform. The only congressional initiative in this area has reinforced the predominant role of the states. In 1975 federal legislation was enacted that would provide funds to encourage the states to develop and implement school finance equalization plans.

Congress's position is not surprising when viewed historically. Education is legally a state function since the Constitution did not delegate it to the federal government. This has been a major reason why the federal role in education has always been limited. There has been an ongoing debate about the extent to which the federal government should become involved in elementary and secondary education. While this issue was briefly resolved in the compromises that made ESEA possible, it has not been permanently settled.

2. *The second avenue for federal redress would have followed a Supreme Court decision declaring the current system of financing education in this country unconstitutional.* That possibility was eliminated in 1973 by the Court's decision in *San Antonio Independent School District v. Rodriguez*[4] that a child's right to public education is not a "fundamental [federal] right" under the Fourteenth Amendment. However, the Court suggested that while Texas school finance arrangements did not violate the Fourteenth Amendment of the U.S. Constitution, it was possible that numerous states had constitutions that explicitly guaranteed a child's right to an education. Thus a federal institution (the Supreme Court) by a negative act played a very explicit role in strengthening the role of state government in educational finance.

3. *Another national decision by the President, while not directly related to education, strengthened the hand of state governments.* President Ford's decision in 1975 not to intervene in New York City's fiscal crisis with long-term aid or guarantees of debt instruments signaled to all local governments that states must first help their cities before they could expect aid from the federal government.

The State Arena

Developments at the federal level have not aided those trying to achieve more equitable systems for financing schools. Greater success has been realized at the state level. More than a dozen states in the early 1970s adopted new state education-aid formulas designed to further the goal of equalization.[5]

One factor contributing to state actions was a series of court decisions. Beginning with the Supreme Court of California in the *Serrano* case of 1971, a number of state and federal courts have found systems of raising revenues for education unconstitutional. The U.S. Supreme Court in the narrow five-to-four *Rodriguez* decision (referred to earlier) ruled that the Fourteenth Amendment of the U.S. Constitution does not prohibit states from utilizing systems that rely primarily on the local property tax base to finance public schools. However, courts in California, Kansas, New Jersey, and Connecticut have found that their state constitutions prohibit such systems of funding. In other states, the threat of court action and the logic of these court decisions have prompted citizens' commissions and public officials to consider changes in the financing of public schools.

The state debates have focused on two basic issues: how to raise the revenue to finance a new aid formula and how to distribute the resulting funds among local school districts. A major component in these discussions has been traditional arguments about the merits of decentralization versus centralization.

Reformers have maintained that existing systems, with their great differences in expenditures based on local property wealth, could not be justified and that the only way to remedy the deficiencies was a greater state role, by the state either providing a larger proportion of school revenues or redistributing locally raised funds from relatively wealthy to poorer districts.

Others have argued that a greater state role would reduce local control of education. The greater uniformity that it would produce would be that of mediocrity rather than excellence. In addition, such centralization would discourage innovation and result in educational programs that were not responsive to local conditions, desires, and needs.

The extent to which the fears of those opposing equalization plans have been realized have depended on the nature of the new formula enacted in each state. In general, for poorer school districts, the new plans have expanded local options since previously their limited tax bases had severely constrained local decision making on educational matters. In addition, in most cases only the revenue-raising function has become more centralized, but expenditure decisions (both about the total level of expenditures and their composition) have been left at the level of the local district. The exceptions have been those states that have imposed ceilings on local tax rates or on the rate at which expenditures can grow from year to year.[6]

To some extent, the critics who complained that the new systems in their uniformity and simplicity would not be sufficiently sensitive to the needs of individual school districts were correct. Both the old equalization formulas adopted prior to 1970 and those adopted in this decade made state aid an inverse function of the local district's ability to finance its schools from local resources. The basic indicator of local fiscal ability in the formulas was local property wealth per pupil.

Typically, cities appear wealthy when such a measure of fiscal ability is used, and they receive less equalization aid than many suburban and rural districts. Not only do cities have substantial commercial and industrial property to raise the tax rolls but in addition they have fewer public school children relative to their total population than most districts because of higher proportions of the elderly and higher enrollments in private and parochial schools.

Cities have argued they are shortchanged by such measures of fiscal capacity on a number of grounds. They maintain city school districts have greater educational needs than less urban districts with comparable tax bases. Disadvantaged, handicapped, and non-English-speaking students, who have greater educational needs and are more expensive to educate, are concentrated in a disproportionate fashion in big cities. The cities have also argued that the costs of providing the same education to average students is higher in cities than elsewhere. Finally, there is the "municipal overburden" argument, that cities do and must provide a much greater array of municipal services than other localities. As a result, education constitutes a much smaller proportion of the local government budget than in other types of jurisdictions. A correspondingly smaller proportion of the local tax base is available to finance education in cities. Many argue it is unrealistic to use the total tax base per pupil to compare the local resources available to finance education in localities where education constitutes 85 percent of the local government budget with those where it constitutes 30 percent.

Some of the more recently adopted equalization formulas have used more sophisticated measures of local wealth in trying to be sensitive to variations in local conditions. Two attempts to deal with the problems of the cities and those of other districts as well have been to incorporate personal income into the wealth measure and to use per capita rather than per pupil wealth measures. Thus while the earlier formulas may have suffered from a lack of sensitivity to local needs and resources, subsequent refinements may have reduced that problem and future developments are likely to go further in this direction.

The development of new sophisticated and sensitive aid formulas has not settled the issue of the relationship between the financing and the governance of education. Unfortunately, there has been very little empirical research in this area. The available evidence suggests that control does not necessarily rest with the level of government providing the funds. The funding agency often has little control over the use of its monies. This may be particularly true for education due to the strong local control tradition.[7] However, these findings have also been reported in studies of other functions. Astrid E. Merget reported in a study of welfare reform that despite the fact that in 1967 the federal and state governments together provided almost 90 percent of total welfare costs, tremendous local variations occurred in implementing federal and state formulas.[8]

The Politics of School Finance at the State Level

At the state level it has been state legislatures that have emerged as the dominant policymakers in educational finance. The legislatures' movement to center stage on school finance issues is a relatively new phenomenon. Until very recently it was state education departments that took the lead in this area. A factor contributing to the legislatures' increased role has been the court decisions referred to earlier. In most states, a new, more equalizing school finance formula required passage of additional legislation. There have been two primary routes through which new school finance laws have been initiated, the state legislature and referenda. As the interest in school finance reform has intensified in recent years, proponents of change have tried both routes. They have been more successful in the state legislatures.

Scholars have studied attempts to adopt new formulas following both routes. Their research indicates the central role of state legislatures in attempts to change the methods of financing public education. In addition, because the studies focus on basic elements of the political process, their findings may apply to attempts to change policy outside the realm of school finance.[9]

There appear to be both considerable similarities and striking differences in the variables that affect the fate of school finance measures processed through state legislatures or through the referendum procedure. Four factors seem to operate in the same fashion in both arenas: compromise, political leadership, the impact of events outside the normal sphere of educational politics, and the state fiscal context.

Compromise, Leadership, and Atypical Events

A measure in which the major issues had been previously worked out among the various interested parties stood a much better chance of passage than one where such compromises had not been worked out and the proposal represented only one point of view. Furthermore, the likelihood of passage was greater if one or more political leaders adopted school finance as an issue and played an active role in the movement for change. Both state legislators and governors played such a leadership role in different states.

While the existence of both compromise and political leadership increased the chances of success, neither was sufficient to ensure it. Proposals where one or both elements were present were defeated. Another factor that was a necessary but not a sufficient condition for adoption of a new formula was developments outside the normal pattern of educational decision making. These included the court suits, the efforts of national groups (e.g., the Education Commission of the States, the National Education Finance Project, and the National Lawyers Committee for Civil Rights under Law), and the appointment of special state commissions to study school finance.

The State Fiscal Context

Most proposals for equalizing local school expenditures involve increases in the state level of funding for education. In trying to reduce the disparities in local expenditures, one could try to reduce the differences between high- and low-spending districts by raising the expenditures of the latter, reducing those of the former, or both. For obvious political reasons, public officials are unlikely to support either the second or third alternative. Thus most proposals call for the "leveling up" of expenditures in poorer districts and hence require additional state funds (or else the redistribution of local revenues from rich to poor districts, which is also politically unpopular).

It is this need for additional state monies for education that makes the state's fiscal context important. If a state has the revenue to finance a new aid system, then the conflicts and politics related to changing the school finance system are much simpler because they focus almost exclusively on the distribution question. On the other hand, if new revenues must be raised, then the conflict involves both the revenue and distribution questions.

In the five states that held referenda in 1972-73, it was not apparent in any of them that there was money available to finance a new system. As a result, the way in which the additional revenues were to be raised became a major matter of debate in each state. Where legislatures adopted new plans, in all but one state no new taxes or increases in taxes were needed to support the new aid system; funds were available for this purpose from state surpluses or revenue sharing monies. Therefore, many potential issues were avoided in those states.

Where additional revenues are necessary to fund a new system, the current state tax structure also appears to be important. The problem becomes even greater if the state has only one of the two major state taxes, sales and income. Politically, it is usually easier to raise the level of an existing tax than to impose a new one. As a general rule, people do not like to acquire new taxes; they prefer those they have already experienced. In addition, in states that have only a sales or an income tax, the rates on that tax as well as for other state taxes and fees are likely to be rather high to compensate for the lack of the other major tax. This makes it more difficult to raise the rates on existing taxes. In such states, the debate over school finance may become subordinated to the conflict over state taxes. This appeared to happen in several states that conducted referenda, as well as in New Jersey, where the legislature was stalemated over the revenue issue.

Differences between the Two Arenas

Two major differences marked the experiences in the two arenas. The first was simply the likelihood of success using the two routes. Chances of changing the school finance system were far less likely if a referendum was used than if the legislature was the final decision maker.

A number of factors seemed to contribute to the lack of success via the referenda, particularly if the measure was put on the ballot through the initiative process. A major reason was that the referendum and initiative processes appeared to deter the compromise that was previously mentioned as being so crucial. Usually, such measures are framed by a single sponsor (or a very small group of interests) who circulates the petition to put it on the ballot and consults with other interested parties to elicit their support only after the issue is already on the ballot. There is little or no attempt to build a coalition and compromise the matter prior to placing it on the ballot. Even when the legislature puts a measure on the ballot, there is less incentive to fully compromise than there is if the legislature has the final say.

In addition, the statistics on state constitutional referenda reveal that (1) fiscal matters are less likely to be adopted than ones dealing with nonfiscal matters, and (2) measures proposed by the initiative process are rarely adopted.[10] Initiatives fare so badly in part because they tend to be controversial issues, ones that have either been rejected by the legislature or which the proponent thinks the legislature would not endorse. All these referenda dealt with fiscal concerns, and nearly all were proposed by initiatives.

The second difference between the two processes was the role played by the complexity of the reform measure. In the legislature, it was desirable to have a complex measure, one with a number of features and elements. The multiplicity of ingredients was a means of building support for the entire proposal by accommodating a variety of diverse interests. Typically, the final measure incorporated a number of topics that at least on the surface appeared unrelated to equalization. However, these additional features were crucial to the bill's success because in most states there were not sufficient votes to pass a straight equalization measure.

The referenda posed a very different situation. All the proposals were very complex, they had a number of components, and in this instance, their complexity may have contributed to their defeat. In part because they had not been compromised before they appeared on the ballot, the multiplicity of features made it easy to develop a negative coalition, one against rather than for the proposals. A group or individual only had to find one aspect of the proposal they strenuously objected to, and they would oppose the entire measure. As a result, on each referendum nearly every major interest group who took a stand on the issue opposed it, most for quite different reasons. Support for the proposal usually was limited to the one or two groups that had initially proposed the referendum.

Simplicity might have helped the referenda proposals since another effect of their complicated nature was that many voters were confused about them, especially in light of the conflicting claims of the opposing camps. Fiscal issues are difficult to explain to the general public under any conditions, and the complexity of these measures increased that problem. The confusion and its impact could be seen in public opinion polls taken during some of the referenda campaigns. The proportion of voters saying they had no opinion or did not know how they would vote increased as the election drew closer. On election day, it appeared that such individuals voted no, preferring the familiar (the current system) to the unknown. In addition, the numerous uncompromised features simply made it easier to build a negative coalition because there were so many aspects that one of them was bound to offend someone's interests.

The difference in the role of complexity in these two arenas may indicate that in some respects their political processes are dissimilar. Logrolling—exchanging a vote on one issue for support on another—is a major part of legislative politics. Thus one builds support by adding more features to a legislative proposal, but similar complexity on a referendum issue may confuse and alienate the voters and aid the opposition. In part, these differences reflect the fact that the complexity in a legislative proposal may represent a set of tradeoffs and compromises, while it usually does not in the case of a referendum.

Subsequent events in the states that held referenda in 1972 or 1973 provide additional evidence of the greater likelihood of the enactment of a new formula if the legislative route is pursued. In two of the five states, the next legislative session considered the issue of school finance and adopted new school-aid formulas. In a third state the referenda route was tried again, and a new measure was rejected by the public. Both strategies were utilized in one state; the legislature passed a modest new proposal, and a measure put on the ballot by the governor was defeated.

Events in the 1973-75 period also point to the importance of the fiscal context to school finance reform. In the last 12 to 18 months, little has been accomplished because the revenue to finance new plans has been lacking. States generally have not had surpluses, and their revenue-sharing funds have already been committed to other areas. During the same period no state has implemented a substantial new school-aid formula. In fact, the combined impact of inflation and recession has meant that at least three states that had enacted new formulas in the early 1970s have been unable to continue fully funding those formulas.

In this period of fiscal difficulties for state and local governments, states have essentially fallen into three categories with regard to their actions on school finance—no activity in this area, examination of the problem without substantive action, or adoption of a new formula without substantial funding for it.

The Future

In general, recent events suggest that the parameters of the debate about school finance may change considerably in the future. Three factors will severely restrict the way in which the states will approach school finance issues over the next decade. First, the impact of the recession and the state of the economy on costs and revenues will severely restrain the amount of new money available to fund new equalization programs. The increasing tightness in state and local government budgets will mean severe competition for funds among all functions, including education. In the next few years, the politics of school finance reform may focus increasingly on the revenue rather than the distribution questions.

Second, many expect the decline in school enrollments to lead to a reduction or stabilization in education budgets. Great political pressure will develop to reduce aid in light of enrollment declines rather than taking advantage of lower pupil-teacher ratios to improve the quality of education.

Third, the near default of the city of New York may restrain future borrowing by school districts. Local governments need to borrow for two reasons. First, they issue bonds (long-term debt instruments) to build facilities (e.g., schools). Second, they may issue notes (short-term debt instruments) for "cash flow" or personal borrowing needs. The latter need is a result of erratic revenue patterns. State and federal aid and locally raised taxes often come at irregular periods. Teachers and other school personnel must be paid regularly, not simply when the money arrives. To overcome low-cash periods, local budget officials borrow short term by issuing notes (until recently at low interest rates) in anticipation of future taxes or aid. The notes are purchased by financial institutions such as banks and resold to individuals or other institutions. A major factor leading to New York's crisis was that the city issued notes when it knew no aid or tax revenues were forthcoming.

Like all investors, those who buy notes are concerned about the safety of their investment. New York's misuse of short-term borrowing may well lead municipal investors, particularly individual investors, to search for other places to put their money despite the tax-free (interest) aspect of a school district's debt.

The narrowing of the market is also the result of other events that are quite independent of the New York situation. As Table 3-3 demonstrates, 1975 was an extremely heavy year for municipal borrowing. In the last eight years, short-term borrowing has quadrupled while long-term debt has doubled. This has meant greater competition than ever before for such funds. For large districts that depend heavily on the municipal financial market for seasonal borrowing needs, it may mean higher interest rates or at the least more competition.

Just as importantly, "who buys bonds" has also changed dramatically during this period. A recent congressional study reported that since 1970 there has been a decline in the proportion of the market represented by commercial banks (see Table 3-4). This is a particular problem for the short-term market, where the large commercial banks are substantial investors. There are many reasons for the reduced interest of the large commercial banks. In part, they no longer need tax-exempt bonds because of recent setbacks in their real estate

Table 3-3
Volume of Municipal Borrowing, 1967-1975

(Amounts Are Par Values in Millions of Dollars)

Year	Long-term	Short-term	Total
1967	14,300	8,000	22,300
1968	16,300	8,600	24,900
1969	11,700	11,700	23,400
1970	18,888	17,811	35,999
1971	25,006	26,259	51,265
1972	23,748	24,705	49,018
1973	23,957	24,705	48,662
1974	24,317	29,543	53,860
1975[a]	30,124	33,932	64,056

[a]Annual rate based on January-June volume.

Source: Reprinted from *The Causes of New York City's Fiscal Crisis* (Washington, D.C.: Congressional Budget Office, October 1975), Table 1.

Table 3-4
Annual Net Changes in Holdings of Municipal Securities by Major Holder Groups (1970-1975)

(Amounts Are Par Values in Billions of Dollars)

Holder	1970	1971	1972	1973	1974	1975[a] First Quarter	Second Quarter
Commercial banks	10.7	12.6	7.2	5.7	5.5	− 2.7	6.9
Households	− 0.8	− 0.2	1.0	4.3	10.0	13.9	9.3
All other[b]	1.3	5.2	6.2	3.7	1.9	2.9	4.5
Total	11.2	17.6	14.4	13.7	17.4	14.0	20.7

[a]Annual rate.

[b]This includes corporate business, state and local general funds, mutual savings banks, insurance companies, state and local government retirement funds, and brokers and dealers.

Source: Reprinted from *The Causes of New York City's Fiscal Crisis* (Washington, D.C.: Congressional Budget Office, October 1975), Table 2.

ventures. In addition, the need for more liquidity in their portfolios will force them to diversify their holdings.

The responsibility for dealing with the borrowing needs of school districts also lies with state governments. The federal government has made it clear in its actions on the New York crisis that it will provide only the most minimal aid.

What is suggested here is that major changes in school finance formulas are unlikely to be implemented in the near future for several reasons: because available resources are dwindling; because a new issue—borrowing—may be surfacing (and not simply because of New York); and because the failure to achieve a substantial decision from the nation's highest court will make the state-by-state process more tedious.

On the other hand, the skills and resources of those advocating reform have increased. They have learned to use two new weapons, the courts and sophisticated computer simulations, to further their goals. In addition, the ten years of efforts have produced a substantial number of individuals with considerable experience in the issue, located both in universities and government and in private organizations. Finally, the task of the change advocates is simplified because they can focus their attention on one level of government, the states.

Overview

The developments in school finance in recent years parallel developments in other substantive areas in several respects. For example, the movement away from a heavy reliance on the local property tax is characteristic of the total system of state-local government and not just of school finance. Between 1942 and 1971, the proportion of state-local general revenue from property taxes has declined steadily from 43.5 percent to 26.1 percent.[11] Similarly, the smaller role of local government in financing state and local general expenditures is true in general, not just for education. Furthermore, the state of the economy will have a similar effect on all state and local programs; new funds, expanded programs, or new means of financing are unlikely, and questions of equity will receive less attention as the concern shifts to matters of survival.

In addition, recent years have witnessed the resurgence of state governments in general and state legislatures in particular. School finance appears to be one area in which the legislatures have been able to exert considerable influence.

Several of the trends noted with regard to school finance are ones that seem to characterize other aspects of education. For example, it has been pointed out that the courts have become important on a number of other issues such as desegregation and student rights. Likewise, local control of the public schools is being eroded in most areas of education.[12]

School politics, whether at the local or state level, have always been described as a relatively closed system, dominated by a few élite actors. Therefore, perhaps it is not surprising to find that to change school finance formulas, would-be reformers must work with élite decision makers, the legislators, rather than attempt to bypass them. At least to date, those who have tried to follow a more decentralized strategy involving referenda and mass participation have not been successful.

It is not clear that attempts to achieve reform through this more decentralized route are equally unfruitful in other areas, particularly ones that involve less complex issues and are nonfiscal in nature. However, it is known that amendments to state constitutions proposed through the initiative have much lower adoption rates (9 percent) than those proposed by élite institutions such as the state legislature (67 percent) or the constitutional convention (82 percent).[13]

In conclusion, the major theme in school finance in the past ten years has been one of centralization. Not only has the trend been to greater dependence on state governments for education revenues but, in addition, the major activity with regard to this issue at the state level has been centralized in the state legislature. On the other hand, there is little indication that the system is going to become more centralized in the near future as the result of a greater federal role in this area.

Comments

Joel S. Berke

Professors Shalala and Williams have performed at least three valuable functions in "Political Perspectives on Recent Efforts to Reform School Finance." First, they have provided a concise but comprehensive summary of developments in a policy area that has undergone substantial change during the last five years. They describe the mismatch among taxable resources, tax effort, and fiscal needs in traditional school finance systems and summarize reform alternatives designed to achieve fiscal neutrality and better balance between resources and needs. Their identification of these developments with increased revenue centralization at the state level is a point that seems to be missed by national education interest groups that annually call for a one-third local, one-third state, one-third federal sharing of educational costs long after the states have substantially exceeded this goal and the federal government, at least for the immediate future, has lost all interest in it.

The second function performed by the article is to furnish a political analysis of factors that have contributed to the passage of reform laws and have controlled the speed and quality of change. The analysis of the differential impact of initiative/referendum politics versus legislative politics accords with my own reading of the evidence. And the importance of three other political processes are insightfully identified: the utilization of law suits as a stimulus to reform; the failure of the federal government to assume a leadership role in reforming school finance; and the shift in the development of education-aid formulas and finance systems from state education departments to state legislatures. About those processes, I shall have more to say below.

Third, Professors Shalala and Williams venture a look into the future and suggest that both fiscal prospects and demographic trends augur a continued slowing of the rate and substance of reform in school finance. To some extent, the authors extrapolate from valuable personal experience in this prediction. As central participants in the development of a sweeping reform law in Connecticut, they were to see it adopted in form but, because of the unavailability of adequate funding, to be ignored in substance. This Hobson's choice is, as the authors' analysis implies, likely to be imposed on school finance reformers for at least the short-run future.

Another aspect of the authors' collective personal experience is reflected in the useful discussion of the effect of credit market developments on state and local debt problems and policies. Drawn from Professor Shalala's tour of service as treasurer of New York's "big MAC" emergency finance board, this discussion points to an emerging issue with which scholars and policymakers must wrestle: the politics and policies of state and local debt management.

But because I find myself in substantial agreement with, and in considerable admiration of, "Political Perspectives on Recent Efforts to Reform School Finance," I think the most useful commentary I can provide is to discuss not what the authors said but what they didn't say. Two areas of interest to readers of this book come to mind: first, the impact of political institutions and processes on the substance of policy in current school finance, and, second, the part played by policy research on the development of those policies.

The Influence of Institutions and Processes on School Finance Policy

There are at least three ways in which the institutions and political processes discussed in the article have affected not only the passage or defeat of school finance legislation—the point that Shalala and Williams argue persuasively in their article—but the substantive direction that school finance reform laws have taken as well.

First, from the myriad "equity problems" affecting the raising and distributing of educational revenues—e.g., spending differentials among states, within individual school districts, and among income or ethnic groups—it was the resort to the courts that riveted reformers' attention on one particular problem above all others: wealth-based disparities among districts in educational spending. In the search for the right combination of evidence, precedent, and doctrine to convince the courts, the fiscal neutrality argument (that a state may not constitutionally permit local spending on education to vary with the size of the local tax base) based on the equal-protection clause of federal and state constitutions, proved an early winner. From there it was an easy jump to the conclusion that the legal wrong was the primary policy problem. No wonder, then, that as Shalala and Williams note, "It was this relationship between local property wealth and school expenditures that troubled the new generation of school finance reformers."

But legal remedies derive from effective jurisprudential argumentation, not from the empirical analysis of substantive problems and political interests that produce effective public policies. Thus, for example, the disadvantaged position of urban areas or of children from low-income families and the failure of finance formulas to match resources to educational needs proved unsuccessful in winning law suits. While such concerns have received some attention in the new legislation, "reform" in school finance has been predominantly associated with more effective equalization of property value differentials among districts.

A second aspect of the relationship of political processes to the emphasis on property value equalization derives from another phenomenon identified by Shalala and Williams:

The states won the debate about what level of government should have greater influence over the resources available and the equity of distribution schemes for public education only after efforts to get the federal government to play a major role in this area failed. After ten years of activity in Washington, school finance reformers went back to their state capitals.

Had the federal influence prevailed in school finance reform, it is entirely possible that a different emphasis, more clearly aimed at meeting the educational needs of pupils and the fiscal needs of districts, might have had a more prominent role in the new patterns of distribution. Traditionally, the federal presence in education has focused on the categorical needs of particular sectors of the educational populace and enterprise. Title I of the Elementary and Secondary Education Act, providing as much as 40 percent of federal aid to elementary and secondary education, has successfully targeted funds to hard-pressed urban school districts in ways that no state formulas do. The key to this ability to focus on a major, long-neglected area of state educational finance is the orienting of the Title I aid formula around personal poverty or low income. This insight is only now being incorporated into a few new state aid formulas in relatively rudimentary and preliminary fashion.

That recognition in a few states, however, provides the third impact of the locus of institutional control on the shape of the legislation passed in recent years. As Shalala and Williams observe:

At the state level it has been state legislatures that have emerged as the dominant policymakers in educational finance. The legislatures' movement to center stage on school finance issues is a relatively new phenomenon. Until very recently it was state education departments that took the lead in this area.

The results of this shift in initiative, linked to the need to enact new approaches to school funding that would meet anticipated judicial standards and could attract sufficient legislative support, reflected an attitude that "educational finance is too large and important an issue to leave to musty state education departments." And in the event, that judgment has proved correct. For in perhaps as many as 15 to 20 states as of this writing, substantially revised formulas have been adopted, formulas that reflect in large measure the school finance reform principles of the last five to ten years. True, primary emphasis is on the equalization of the ability of communities to receive more nearly equal revenues for education from equivalent local property tax effort. Yet, in addition, states have tailored their new laws to meet other objectives related to overall tax policy, greater recognition of urban problems, the special needs of pupils in poverty and on welfare, and in some cases, states have junked former state formulas and have adopted new systems based on the writings of the new generation of reformers. The ability of some legislative leaders to make recognizable reform omelettes while minimizing the breaking of eggs were feats deserving of the political *Cordon bleu.* Most notable of the substantive impacts of the legislative rather than education bureaucracy leadership on the issue was the linking of educational reform to more tasty entries on the political menu: property tax-relief and spending limitations. In short, while school finance reform may have retained distinct marks of its judicial origin and the absence of federal sponsorship, the imprint of this new state legislative leadership replaced the marginal annual school finance adjustments that came from the closed deliberations of the state education agency with their favorite local professor of educational administration and the leadership of the state school boards and teachers associations. In place of business-as-usual formula increments came new, legislatively developed school finance systems. These usually contained an important element of continuity, but featured substantially revised provisions to meet the doctrines of the courts, the necessities of mobilizing legislative support for change, and the technical recommendations of the new breed of school finance scholars.

The Influence of Policy Research on School Finance Laws

The influence of those scholars shall be of some interest to readers. Probably in no other major field of domestic policy has the impact of policy research been as influential in the process of change as in school finance. Early formulas of state educational aid had been developed during the first three decades of the century by scholars largely trained in educational administration. Their objectives had been to improve the quality of education in the hinterlands to something nearer that offered in urban centers and to encourage heightened local spending for education particularly in "lighthouse" districts. But during the 1950s and 1960s, economists who specialized in public finance and a few political scientists and educationists with interest in political economy began to note the unforeseen impact of such traditional finance systems: the traditional approaches to school finance were regularly providing disproportionately high revenues to districts of high income, high property value, and suburban location.

Drawing directly on that research, a graduate student at the University of Chicago pursuing doctoral studies in education and law seized on that evidence to suggest a novel theory. In a newsletter for educational administrators, the February 1965 issue of the *Administrator's Notebook*, Arthur Wise wrote:

Most educators are probably aware that, within any state, there are gross inequities in per pupil expenditures. . . . I shall argue that a state, in permitting this inequality to exist, is denying some of its citizens the equal protection of its laws, and is hence acting unconstitutionally. . . . It is the opinion of the present writer that, because of the great discrepancy between per pupil expenditures within many states (which strongly suggests inequality of opportunity), our present systems of educational finance and districting would be found to be unconstitutional.[14]

As refined by subsequent legal scholars, that suggestion was to result, as Professors Shalala and Williams have explained, in a series of courtroom victories for reformers at the state and lower federal court level beginning in 1971. When the U.S. Supreme Court, no longer reflective of the Warren Court philosophy prevalent when Wise wrote, rejected the Fourteenth Amendment argument in the spring of 1973, its action came after the state and lower federal court decisions had had their effect in prodding, directly and indirectly, a number of state legislatures into reform action.

That legislative action, as previously noted, also drew heavily on policy research. As Shalala and Williams note:

. . . the skills and resources of those advocating reform have increased. They have learned to use two new weapons, the courts and sophisticated computer simulations, to further their goals. In addition, the ten years of effort have produced a substantial number of individuals with considerable experience in the issue, located both in universities and government and in private organizations.

These "individuals with considerable experience" have conducted studies for blue-ribbon commissions and legislative committees. They have addressed and worked with groups of policymakers in workshops or conferences convened by groups like the Education Commission of the States and the National Legislative Conference. And they have produced a substantial body of research on problems and alternative solutions that fill the intellectual tool kits of legislative staffers, executive branch analysts, and a growing number of state legislative leaders who have themselves taken the issue seriously enough to develop personal competence in its intricacies.

What have been the characteristics of this research and of the researchers who have conducted it? First, both it and they are a varied lot, drawing on a number of disciplines and types of studies. Analysts with training in political science and public administration have been prominent in their company, as have scholars with graduate degrees and university bases in public finance, business, and educational administration.

Their research has reflected that diversity. At least five types of studies have contributed directly to the formulation of new policy for school funding. First, analyses of fiscal needs and resources that have demonstrated the disparities among communities in taxable capacity, tax burdens, and revenue yields have helped to establish the legislative climate for new laws. Further, scholars have analyzed the particular problems of different regions and pupil populations that have begun to find remedy through special tax treatment for some urban areas or special distributional provisions for high-cost pupils.

Second, policy researchers have illustrated the failure of traditional school finance laws to meet those problems. They have demonstrated why aid formula provisions designed for an era of wealthy central cities and impoverished outlying areas no longer serve the world of the 1970s that has felt the effects of population and economic shifts of substantial proportion. Their work has shown that provisions formally neutral in tone, such as state aid based on proportionately matching local salary levels, provide disproportionately greater aid to wealthy districts able to attract more highly qualified teachers. Or that nominally equalizing-aid formulas frequently have so many limitations in their operation (floors to provide all districts with some aid, ceilings that fall well below the amounts needed to offset local wealth-based disparities, etc.) that in practice the pattern of spending is highly and positively correlated with property valuation per pupil.

Third, these scholars have developed alternative proposals designed to overcome such problems. They have given substance to varied value approaches by providing the technical mechanisms for assuring that states seeking to provide local districts with "equal yield for equal tax effort" will be able to implement their objective, as will states that define equity as "matching educational resources to the needs of different types of pupils" with little regard for local tax rates.

Fourth, as Shalala and Williams note, policy analysts have adapted computer simulation technology to providing information on the likely effects of a variety of potential formulas, thus permitting policymakers to draft legislation with considerably greater knowledge of its tax and distributional effects than has ever been available before. In addition, by merging school finance, general municipal funding, and demographic data sets, policy analysts are able to show the impact of such alternatives on a variety of factors that reach far beyond the basic legislative concern with "how much does my district get" or the simple issue of how much an alternative approach to state aid for education will cost. The impact for income groups, geographic regions, urban/suburban/rural locations, ethnic and racial minorities, and other such questions are available through computer printouts, summary tables, and eventually staff reports.

Finally, while assembling coalitions is the particular province of politicians, policy analysts—both those on public payrolls and those from universities and private organizations—have been known to employ their talents to examine the political systems through which such legislation will both be passed and implemented, with an eye to shaping legislation that will be both substantively sound and politically acceptable. Thus for the dozen or so scholars who have made a specialty of participation in school finance reform, a sensitivity to political reality, a firm grip on quantitative methodological skills, and an ability to move comfortably in both the worlds of research and policy have been the prime stocks in trade.

The authors of the article under discussion are, of course, respected members of that group, and their essay provides evidence that participation in and scholarship about public policy can be mutually supportive activities. To put it another way, "Political Perspectives on Recent Efforts to Reform School Finance" shows that in the field of school finance reform, kissing and telling is appropriate and intellectually valuable behavior.

Notes

1. Frederick M. Wirt and Michael W. Kirst, *The Political Web of American Schools* (Boston: Little, Brown, 1972), pp. 111-114.

2. National Education Association, Research Division, *Estimates of School Statistics, 1974-5* (Washington, D.C., 1975), p. 35.

3. Joel Berke and Michael W. Kirst, *Federal Aid to Education* (Lexington, Mass.: Lexington Books, 1972), pp. 20-46.

4. San Antonio Independent School District *v.* Rodriguez, 411 U.S. 1 (1973).

5. For a description of these state plans, see W. Norton Grubb, *New Programs of State School Aid* (Washington, D.C.: National Legislative Conference, 1974).

6. To some extent the goals of local control and equalization do conflict. Greater equalization is achieved when greater constraints are placed on the choices of local districts about school tax rates and expenditures. The ultimate in equalization is full state assumption where equalization is nearly complete, but local choice about expenditures and taxes is nearly zero.

7. Betsy Levin, Thomas Muller, William J. Scanlon, and Michael Cohen, *Public School Finance: Present Disparities and Fiscal Alternatives.* A Report to the President's Commission on School Finance (Washington, D.C.: The Urban Institute, 1972), p. 248.

8. Astrid E. Merget, "Implications of Welfare Reform for State and Local Government" (unpublished paper, 1972), p. 10.

9. The Syracuse University Research Corporation, financed by the U.S. Office of Education, has examined seven states where legislatures recently passed new school finance formulas. Scholars at Teachers College, Columbia University, under the auspices of The Ford Foundation, have studied the defeats in 1972 and 1973 of referenda that would have reduced or eliminated reliance on the

local property tax to finance education in five states. While the two studies were not designed as a single research undertaking, a comparison of their findings provides considerable insight into the factors contributing to success or failure in attempts to change school finance formulas. The two studies and a comparison of their findings are described in Joel Berke, Donna E. Shalala, and Mary Frase Williams, "Two Roads to School Finance Reform—The One Taken Makes All the Difference," in *Society*, Vol. 14, No. 1.

10. Albert Sturm, "State Constitutions and Constitutional Revision," in *The Book of the States, 1972-73* (Lexington, Ky.: Council of State Governments, 1972), p. 9.

11. Advisory Commission on Intergovernmental Relations, *Significant Features of Fiscal Federalism, 1973-74 Edition* (Washington, D.C.: Government Printing Office, 1974), p. 35.

12. Wirt and Kirst, *The Political Web of American Schools*, pp. 46-49.

13. Sturm, "State Constitutions and Constitutional Revision," p. 4.

14. Arthur E. Wise, "Is Denial of Equal Educational Opportunity Constitutional?," *Administrator's Notebook*, Volume 13, Number 6. The *Administrator's Notebook* is published by the Midwest Administration Center of the University of Chicago.

4

"Don't Trouble Me with the Facts": Congress, Information, and Policy Making for Postsecondary Education

Thomas R. Wolanin

A frequently voiced criticism of the American national government is that it fails to get the best information and analysis available in making decisions or fails to use it when it gets it. This criticism is bolstered by daily reports of blunders: airplanes whose wings crack, a Bay of Pigs invasion that was doomed to failure, a welfare system that provides incentives for dependency and disincentives for work, and a transportation policy that squanders scarce resources and despoils the environment. Most agree that these disasters would not have occurred if the facts at hand had been adequately studied when the critical decisions were made.

Congress among the institutions of the federal government perhaps has been perceived most frequently as making uninformed decisions. The title of a 1965 documentary summarizes this view, "Congress Needs Help."[1] Commentators, scholars, and reformers both inside and outside Congress have long called attention to this problem.[2] For example, most recently the Senate in July 1975 established the independent temporary Commission on the Operation of the Senate "to make a comprehensive and impartial study" of, among other things, "the functioning of Members, officers, and employees of the Senate in the light of the responsibilities of the Senate in the areas of lawmaking, representation and oversight," and also to study "information resources."[3] Senator Culver, the sponsor of the measure creating the commission, characterized it as "a serious attempt to gain better and more rational control over our own affairs."[4] In December 1975 the creation of the independent and privately funded Institute for Congress was announced. Its purpose is to serve as a think tank for the Congress, providing high-quality analysis and policy options in critical areas of public policy.[5]

In the area of federal policy for postsecondary education, the weaknesses of congressional decision making have received particularly harsh comment. For example, in commenting on the 1972 amendments to the Guaranteed Student Loan program, which created administrative chaos and had to be temporarily suspended two months after their enactment, one analyst concludes that "deficiencies in drafting" produced statutory language that was "incomprehensible on its face."[6] The Washington representatives of higher education and academics who pass through the halls of Congress as witnesses or interested

The Spencer Fellowship that I received from the National Academy of Education provided valuable support enabling me to complete this study. I also wish to thank my colleague and friend Larry Gladieux for his perceptive comments and editorial assistance that significantly improved this work.

citizens frequently shake their heads over the apparent irrationality and haphazardness of congressional decision making. It may be that the academic clientele of postsecondary education programs measure the performance of Congress against their standards for assessing the conclusions of scholarly research. Their views might be tempered if congressional processes were compared instead to those of department meetings or faculty senates, where systematic and rational decision making are scarcely the norm.

This essay attempts to provide some preliminary answers to a complex set of questions: Does Congress request and seek the appropriate information in making decisions about higher education policy? Why does Congress frequently not receive the requested information? Why does Congress not use well the information it does get?

Let us begin by assuming that a substantively good decision is one that addresses a legitimate public problem, has the desired impact on that problem, and has few if any unanticipated negative consequences. A good decision-making process is one that brings to bear the available information and analysis in a fairly systematic and orderly fashion. Presumably substantively good decisions are most likely to result from a good decision-making process.

The first requisite for good congressional decision making is gathering and soliciting the best available information and analysis. To get good data you have to ask good questions. Congress gathers much of the information it uses through hearings. Thus the questions and requests for information articulated in hearings are one indicator of whether Congress starts on the right foot in its decision making.

A survey of the recent hearings on postsecondary education legislation indicates that the following four types of questions are predominant:

1. *Clarification.* A large number of questions seek to clarify, highlight and draw out the implications of the recommendations and observations made by witnesses. Questions frequently begin: "Do I understand you to be saying . . . ?" "Is it your intention to . . . ?" or "In other words, you are proposing that . . . ?"[7]

2. *Need.* Questions frequently attempt to document and explore the existence of a public problem to which congressional attention is merited. "How many students are not now attending postsecondary institutions because of their lack of financial resources?" "How many banks have ceased participating in the student loan program because of its administrative complexity or low rates of return?" "How many colleges are in danger of closing their doors for fiscal reasons?" or "How much 'need' for federal financial assistance does a student with a family income of $10,000 have?" are examples of these kinds of questions.[8]

3. *Impact and effects.* Questions are raised concerning the impact of existing programs. Examples would include: "How many students who would

not otherwise be attending postsecondary education are doing so because of federal financial assistance?" "Have the loan cancellation features of the National Direct Student Loan program resulted in teachers being attracted to poverty areas?" or "Are more states engaged in comprehensive planning for postsecondary education as a result of Section 1202?"

Very often the questions try to ascertain the likely effects of proposed legislative changes. These questions are in the general form "If . . . , then . . . ?" For example: "If the eligibility criteria for the College Work Study program are changed, then will students work more to support their education?" "If the rate of return to lenders on student loans is increased, then will more lenders participate in the program?" "If all student loans must be insured in the first instance by state agencies, then will the default rate go down?" or "If the half-cost limitation is removed from the Basic Grant program, then will private colleges and universities be at an unfair disadvantage in competing for students with the publics?"

A variant on the questions dealing with impact of past actions and prospective effects of new legislation are the questions related to state and district concerns of individual House members and senators. These questions are all essentially: "What share will my state (district) get and is this a 'fair' share?" These questions are rarely asked directly. Congressmen seem rather embarrassed to be obvious about the provincialism that is required of them as elected representatives. Statesmanship serving the national interest seems to be the most acceptable public posture. These questions are most often masked beneath general requests for state-by-state breakdowns of data or expressed in directives to the staff.

The questions about impact and effects are essentially questions about means chosen in the past or proposed for the future to attain the objectives that are the heart of the questions relating to public needs and problems.

4. *Cost.* Particularly in recent years in light of the new congressional budget consciousness and frequent presidential vetoes of education bills as inflationary, questions related to "costing-out" proposals have become more prevalent. Committee reports accompanying proposed legislation must now include an "inflation impact" statement. Concern for fiscal implications has crossed the aisle and is no longer the exclusive concern of carping Republicans and conservative Democrats.

Are congressmen asking the questions that would enable them to obtain the information and analysis required for making substantively good decisions with respect to postsecondary education? A review of the hearing records indicates that they are. Congressmen probe to clarify the information and proposals before them. They try to discover public problems that are the legitimate objectives of congressional action. Questions are asked to assess the impact of past decisions as well as to evaluate the probable consequences of options for further action. The fiscal implications of trying to meet a public problem through a particular course of action are addressed. These questions would seem to hold the promise of leading to substantively good decisions and to be rather close to a scheme of cost/benefit analysis.

Congressmen are asking the right questions. But this is only the first step. There do exist very real problems with congressional decision making. The ability of Congress to make good decisions is severely constrained because the questions posed are frequently not answered, or if answers are received, the data are not adequately integrated into the decision-making process. Congress is misunderstood to be sure, and it bears the brunt of the current disenchantment with government at all levels. Congress is a seeming babble of discordant voices and a byzantine maze of committees, subcommittees, and parliamentary proce- dures. But lack of appreciation for the scope and quality of congressional efforts cannot explain away the problem. Nor is the problem simply that congressmen are malevolent, stupid, or inept, at least no more so than the denizens of other American institutions. The issues are far more complex, and unhappily there is no panacea like "throwing the rascals out" or "letting the sunshine in" or "beefing up the staff."

Congress frequently does not get the information it needs or fails to use it when it does for the following five basic reasons:

1. The questions congressmen pose often cannot by their very nature be answered.
2. The internal dynamics and organization of Congress militate in several ways against "good" decision making.
3. Postsecondary education, as an issue arena in which Congress legislates, presents some unique problems.
4. Congress and its sources of information and analysis—the executive branch and the postsecondary education community—have different institutional perspectives and stakes. They frequently talk past rather than to each other.
5. These same providers of information to Congress are limited in their competence to serve congressional needs.

Questions without Answers

Questions from congressmen and requests for information are often quite cogent and well focused on what needs to be known to make a good decision. However, these questions are frequently beyond the ken of rational or scientific inquiry. Most importantly they relate to the future behavior of human beings in a society. It is neither feasible nor appropriate to subject citizens to the experimental conditions that would enable one to make scientific predictions related to the most relevant questions. You cannot isolate people from all the random influences of life for a sufficiently long period to permit scientifically verifiable conclusions. For example, it would seem repugnant to democratic sensibilities to examine the impact of the Special Services for the Disadvantaged program by carefully monitoring and controlling the activities of recipients to screen out any assistance they might receive other than through this program.

In a democratic society it is also not possible to provide the benefits of a program to one group of citizens while withholding them from another group that will serve as an experimental control group. You could not, as a practical political matter, for example, investigate the important question of how many students were induced to enroll in higher education through the availability of basic grants by making them available to some while denying them to a carefully matched control group—which is to say that you cannot treat citizens like bacteria in a petri dish.

Given this happy limitation, social scientists have not done very well in predicting human behavior. Even on a subject as circumscribed as voting behavior, the state of the predictive art is still rather crude. When the question relates to the impact of proposed legislative changes, decision makers operate in the realm of informed guesswork. Higher education legislation seeks to provide incentives and disincentives, opportunities and prohibitions that will result in people living differently and presumably better by some standard of public welfare. Whether more states would in fact plan or award financial-aid grants, whether more banks would make student loans, or whether fewer students would default on loans as a result of proposed changes in the law are questions that generally can only bring forth anecdotal observations, folk wisdom, or unwarranted leaps of inference from the available data.[9]

The inability of social science to answer the important questions about impact and effects indicates that when the ends are agreed on, there are no easy formulas to choose among alternative means. When the problem is to choose the correct objectives or goals, policymakers are even less able to call on the analysts for the answers. Since the demise of natural law, it is generally agreed that questions of values and preferences cannot be resolved solely by rational analysis. Which should claim higher priority in public policy, the plight of the middle class or the poor? How much of the independence and autonomy of higher education institutions should be sacrificed to eradicate racism and sexism on the campuses? On such issues policymakers must rely on their judgment and their values.[10]

The fact that legislators cannot follow the model of research scientists or the ideal of rational-comprehensive decision making does not condemn them to making choices with a coin toss, a Ouija board or tarot cards. They can make informed choices based on the best available information. They can get answers to their questions in the sense of responses, but they cannot get answers in the sense of definitive determinations. The following discussion focuses on the constraints that prevent congressmen from becoming as well informed as possible, leaving aside the will-o'-the-wisp of ultimate answers.

The Internal Dynamics of Congress

Congress fails to get or to use the best information and analysis for a number of important reasons related to the organization, processes, and style of congressional operations.

1. As the scope of federal activity has increased in the postdepression, postwar era, members of Congress have been stretched ever thinner over the continuously broadening gamut of issues demanding their attention. Not only are there more issues but they have become more complex as federal policy seeks to intervene in intricate webs of domestic and international relations, for example, with issues like national health insurance or the regulation of multinational corporations. Added to this is the knowledge explosion that showers reams and tomes on each facet of every problem. In addition, congressmen are more accessible to their more mobile and sophisticated constituents, their constituents increasingly expect that congressmen will spend their spare moments in their home districts, and the constituents have a growing need for assistance in coping with the staggeringly complex array of federal programs. Thus we have more issues, more complex issues, more information about each issue, more competing demands on the legislator's time, but the same number of congressmen.

Good policy-making decisions today require the integration of vast amounts of information and great care to avoid inadvertently swamping innocent bystanders with the ripples of policy choices. They require sustained attention and reflection. Yet uninterrupted time to think about policy problems is what the legislators least possess.[11] The scarcity of time is particularly acute in the Senate, where 100 persons span the same national agenda that is divided among 435 in the House. A senator's briefing on a major issue may often consist of a "walkie," listening to a staff aide while walking the distance between the office door and the elevator. Senator Dirksen once observed:

I would not dare to say to the people of Illinois that I knew all the things that go on. . . . To do so I would really need roller skates to get from one subcommittee to another, without even then knowing everything about every subject matter which is considered by the various committees.[12]

There are too many issues and the members have too little time. The usual nostrum of increasing the congressional staff or support services does not address the issue. The staff plays an important role in doing the pick-and-shovel work and organizing the information and options. But they are not elected, and there is no substitute in a democratic system for the judgment of the people's elected representatives on questions of public policy. To their credit, members of Congress generally do not abdicate to the staff, but they often do make slipshod and ill-informed decisions.

The solution is to either give the members more time for policy thinking or to reduce the number of issues they must deal with. Many suggestions have been offered to free up more time for the central task of lawmaking, for example, four-year terms for House members or a reduction in the number of quorum calls and recorded votes. Increased specialization has also been suggested with the members becoming experts on narrower sets of issues. Then Congress could operate by deferring to sophisticated experts on each issue. This is largely the way the congressional system now operates, and increased specialization and reciprocity carry with them the risk that decisions with a national impact will not be made with either the legitimacy or quality that comes from scrutiny by the national legislature.

On the other side of the coin, reducing the number of issues, one possibility suggests itself particularly in the postsecondary education arena. Congress undertook continuous oversight as a major responsibility with the Legislative Reorganization Act of 1946 in response to the increasing delegation of policy-making authority to the executive branch as the federal government forged out into broad new areas of social welfare, economic regulation, and international relations. One manifestation of the commitment to oversight was a trend toward limited authorizations that provide regular deadlines requiring congressional reexamination of programs in the process of reauthorizing them. A result of this has been an artificial workload as programs that no one has any problems with are automatically cast up before the Congress.

The postsecondary education programs created by the National Defense Education Act of 1958, the Higher Education Facilities Act of 1963, and the Higher Education Act of 1965 have all been in place for a decade or more and have all been reauthorized at least twice. Many of these programs, like College Work Study or the Title II Library programs, are ticking along quite smoothly. There is no reason why they ought not to be permanently authorized.

Permanent authorization does not imply permanent commitment. Programs can be amended, restructured, or abolished at any time. Selective permanent authorizations would mean an end to the automatic workload dictated by statutory expirations rather than perceived public needs. Permanent authorizations might also improve some programs by enhancing their stability since the temptation to tinker with them when they expire would not be presented to Congress.

Permanently authorizing some postsecondary education programs would permit the relevant committees to focus on problems as they arise or to undertake their oversight on a program-by-program basis rather than having the entire potpourri of programs dumped on them every few years.[13] One criticism of such a revised approach to handling postsecondary education is that it would sacrifice the "conceptual overview" that the committees now can take as all the programs expire together. The committees do not take such an overview now in part because the programs directly and indirectly related to postsecondary education are scattered in the jurisdictions of dozens of subcommittees. The House Subcommittee on Postsecondary Education and the Senate Education Subcommittee fall far short of encompassing postsecondary education programs in their ambit. Their efforts even with respect to those programs in their purview are currently usually less than a model of systematic conceptual thinking. Finally, there is no reason why changes limited to problem areas of a single program at a time could not be conceptually related to some general strategy of public policy objectives. Nor is there any reason why a broad reconceptualization and across-the-board review could not be undertaken as dictated by new priorities, a fresh administration, or social changes.

2. Policy decisions in Congress are made not only in the context of the general time constraints noted previously but also in specific settings not especially conducive to careful analysis and systematic use of information. Formal congressional decisions are made at three points in the congressional process: committee mark-ups, floor amendment and passage, and House-Senate conference committees. Decisions in these contexts are often preceded by careful staff work, thorough homework by the members, and long periods of thoughtful informal discussions and negotiations among the principles involved in a given issue. But once it comes time to actually make the decisions, a new cast of characters becomes involved: all the committee members or members of the House or Senate as a whole. Many of them are only marginally interested in or informed about the issues. While they will generally defer to the experts (especially if the recognized experts present a solid front), they may be swayed by the passions of a particularly hot issue or the appeal of popular cliches and "buzz words."

The debates on higher education policy in 1969-1972 were dominated first by campus unrest and then school busing. These issues soaked up the time, energy, and commitment of the participants, leaving many difficult substantive issues starved for attention. The federal student-aid grant proposals of both Presidents Eisenhower and Kennedy succumbed to the cliches that gift aid "saps initiative" and that "nobody should get a free ride."

In committees and on the floor, the objective is to get unanimity if possible or at least 50 percent plus one in support of one's policy position. Usually the interested and expert carry the day. But often there is disagreement among the experts or difficult questions from the novices. These challenges must be met as the clock ticks toward zero in the time for debate under the rules on the floor or as the committee chairman anxiously pushes for a decision before a quorum slips away. Amendments, suggestions, and objections must be dealt with by quick, instinctual, and pragmatic judgments in many cases. Choices are made often with an eye to achieving accommodation. What the exact impact of an amendment might be and how it fits with other parts of a bill or existing law and practice is less important than that it does not look too bad, and its acceptance will buy a crucial increment of support or silence a troublesome critic. For example, the decisions concerning the needs test in the Guaranteed Student Loan program were made during a marathon 15-hour session of a House-Senate conference pushing to report out a bill. This issue was a stubborn clump of underbrush that needed to be cleared away before the legislators could confront the antibusing amendments that threatened to sink the entire enterprise.

Irving Janis has developed the concept of "groupthink" to describe a psychological syndrome in small groups of decision makers that distorts their perceptions and judgments and results in poor decisions.[14] Janis's analysis is particularly applicable to bureaucratic decision making and foreign policy decisions. However, an analogous phenomenon can be observed in congressional decision-making settings. Once a decision has been reached in the heat of battle, there is a strong feeling that one ought not to investigate its merits any further, at least not until another stage in the process is reached where it can be "perfected." To examine the consequences and implications of a political accommodation might reveal practical flaws that make the decision untenable. Then the agreement would have to be scrapped and a painful subject reopened. The political process of accommodation would have to start over. As the epic conference on the Education Amendments of 1972 ground on, Chairman Perkins increasingly focused with single-minded determination on reaching agreement on a bill. His job as chairman was to get agreement. He repeated over and over, "We're gonna get a bill." As he drove the conference, the practical problem of implementing the agreements receded to secondary importance in the face of the fact that agreements had been reached. Nagging doubts about the merits were submerged in a conspiracy of silence. Indeed, the rules and norms of the Congress make it difficult to "reconsider" decisions, indicating a general institutional bias against reopening past decisions.

Political calculations in the decision-making arenas sometimes dictate tactics expressly designed to minimize discussion and the ability to bring information and analysis to bear. A common tactic for pressing a policy position is to draft an amendment, circulate it to all who might be interested both within Congress and among the affected clientele, and try to generate as broad a consensus as possible. Another tactic is to quietly put together a proposal and spring it as an amendment in committee or on the floor, trusting in surprise, one's own superior preparation, and the pressures to move the bill to carry the day. These surprise packages often are not subject to probing analysis or careful scrutiny. Developed in isolation, they frequently contain limitations and practical implications that are undesirable even from the point of view of their sponsor.

A notable example is the Buckley Amendment. A floor amendment offered by Senator Buckley of New York to the 1974 Elementary and Secondary Education Act, it was primarily intended to provide access for parents to their children's school records in elementary and secondary schools and to preclude the use of this information in ways that would infringe on the privacy of students and their parents. As an apparent afterthought, students in post-secondary education were given the same rights as parents. The result was a period of chaos in postsecondary education as the ramifications of the amendment for admissions and job placement recommendations and in other areas were sorted out. Senator Buckley by his own admission did not intend the broad unsettling impact of his amendment on postsecondary education.[15] An opportunity for the postsecondary education community to comment on the amendment would have probably revealed its disruptive potential and resulted in some modifications to preserve its salutory impact while mitigating the trauma.

3. Congress is not hierarchical. Power is diffused among committees, elected party leaders, party caucuses, ideological and geographical groupings, and informal networks of affinity. When the executive branch sends a message to Congress, it has normally been formulated by drawing on the relevant program people at the bureau level, circulating drafts to all who are interested within the executive branch and reviewing the final statement at the cabinet and presidential levels. The executive branch speaks formally with one coordinated voice. A presidential message and a congressional request for information are not parallel. A congressional request can come from any of the multiple centers of congressional power down to and including the individual member, who in the final analysis has a vote and is rarely subject to discipline because his tenure in the legislature rests on his personal standing with his constituents and is beyond the reach of congressional leaders. To return to an earlier point, questions from members of Congress are often good questions aimed at eliciting the information relevant for good decision making. But the questions frequently get lost in the cacophony of congressional inquiries. Looked at in sum, the questions may add up to a rational inquiry, but viewed in the context of a diffuse and decentralized legislative body, they look more like a confetti storm. Congress does not ask questions; many members of Congress in a variety of positions with different goals and timetables do.

In addition, as the members bounce like pinballs between all their obligations and responsibilities, they frequently lose track of their own inquiries. Sustained interest and follow up are relatively rare. Today's interesting point is superseded by tomorrow's crisis.

Finally, the diffuse and decentralized inquiries from congressional sources necessarily mean that the responses are as widely scattered as the questions. There are certainly efforts to disseminate significant studies that result from an inquiry by one member or one committee. For example, the General Accounting Office and the Congressional Research Service frequently circulate to all members lists of their recent research reports that anyone interested can obtain.

But the lack of congressional hierarchy results in the absence of a mechanism to integrate all of the relevant information related to a given problem that is scattered all over Capitol Hill.[16]

4. An increasingly common technique for legislating in a policy arena is via omnibus bills. These massive bills collect in separate titles as many as 20 or 30 loosely related measures all dealing generally with the same subject. They are an effective device for increasing congressional efficiency as related subjects are all processed through the legislative mill in a single batch. They also have the potential at least for providing the opportunity to take an overview of a large part of the legislation having an impact on a particular policy arena.

But omnibus bills also mitigate against good decision making on the merits of issues in two important ways. First, in any collection of titles, some will always be more significant and controversial than others. Naturally, attention and effort will focus on these key sections of the bill. The result is that the less visible and less controversial parts of the bill will slip through the process with little sustained scrutiny. Possible problems or defects in these areas pale in significance compared to the "big" issues and fall through the cracks in the congressional process.

For example, in the field of postsecondary education, attention in the consideration of omnibus bills is usually focused on the Title IV student financial-aid programs. The other titles such as Developing Institutions are encompassed by the rubric "the rest of the Higher Education Act." In the case of the Developing Institutions programs, a sharp but largely underground controversy exists concerning the very nature of the programs (What is a "developing institution?"), the federal responsibility toward these institutions (When, if ever, should developing institutions be reasonably expected to become "developed?"), and the executive branch strategy for implementing this title (large grants to a few institutions versus a broader distribution of the funds). But these issues have never been thoroughly aired before Congress because they are always overshadowed by other more crucial questions.

Second, omnibus bills are an effective technique for building political support. By a process of logrolling, all committee members with a pet idea related to postsecondary education can find a home for it under the broad umbrella of the omnibus bill. Thus all interested members of the committee or subcommittee are given a personal stake in the bill. The essence of logrolling is: "I'll take yours if you'll take mine." The necessary corollary of it is: "I won't question yours if you won't question mine." Such an attitude without a doubt lubricates the congressional wheels, but it is hardly conducive to probing inquiry.

In 1971 Mrs. Green's postsecondary subcommittee in the House was composed on the Democratic side largely of chairmen of other subcommittees. They had little time to spare for higher education issues. Mrs. Green got the support of most of them for her bill by accepting their special programs as titles.

John Dent of Pennsylvania had Mineral Conservation Education; Roman Pucinski of Illinois, Ethnic Heritage Studies; Dominick Daniels of New Jersey, Youth Camp Safety; and Philip Burton of California, land grant status for the College of the Virgin Islands and the University of Guam. None of these programs was reviewed very carefully, and the Youth Camp Safety title illustrates how far an omnibus bill can be stretched to accommodate all who are needed on board.

5. Congressional decisions are made in an adversary system. Interested and affected parties, pro and con, rather than disinterested but informed observers, dominate the schedule of witnesses. Committee reports provide the option for concurring and dissenting views. The time for floor debate is divided between proponents and opponents.

An adversary system places a premium on building your side of the argument as vigorously as possible. While there are strong norms against falsifying or grossly distorting data, shading and selectivity to bolster one's case are accepted. It is left for the opponents to discover the weak links and to provide a compensating shading that blends with the other side to provide a hue approximating reality. While such a system is fundamental to policy making in a democracy, it has obvious limitations in contrast to the ideal models of disinterested research and rational-comprehensive decision making.

In addition, in Congress this method has unique limits. In the judicial model of an adversary system, the disputants offer evidence and arguments through their advocates to an impartial arbitrator, who then reaches a decision on the basis of the evidence and the criteria stipulated for deciding by the law. In the congressional context there are clearly no stipulated criteria for deciding what is desirable public policy. There are rarely even stipulated goals or objectives for policy on the basis of which criteria for making decisions could at least theoretically be developed. Each congressional decision maker weighs arguments and information against his own policy objectives and his own criteria for deciding whether those objectives will be advanced by a particular course of action. Thus a discussion of congressional "intent," as if it were a discoverable single thing, has a distinctly surreal quality. Administrators and judges must often inevitably insert their own preferences in implementing and construing statutes as the pursuit of the grail of congressional intent is rarely conclusive.

Furthermore, in the congressional process there is no impartial arbiter. Members of Congress have state, district, party, ideological, and personal goals to advance. They are active participants in the adversary process as both advocates and decision makers. Thus the adversary process is skewed by the power of those congressmen who can influence the course of events in each decision-making forum. For example, a subcommittee chairman might schedule witnesses most sympathetic to his view at a prime time when many other members can attend. Uncongenial witnesses will be put on while the bells are ringing for votes and the members are scurrying to and from the floor. Alice Rivlin had produced as

Assistant Secretary for Planning and Evaluation of HEW a report advocating student aid as the fundamental strategy for supporting higher education. Mrs. Green, who was more sympathetic to institutional aid, scheduled Rivlin as the last witness on a busy day, took her testimony, and concluded the hearing after brief questioning.[17]

Higher Education as an Issue Arena

As a subject to be encompassed by analysis and as an object of federal policy, postsecondary education presents some unique difficulties for congressional decision makers that inhibit their ability to be well informed about it. First, as noted above, responsibility for policy affecting postsecondary education is widely scattered across the federal landscape. There are nearly 400 separate programs of support for postsecondary education administered by more than 20 federal agencies.[18] Approximately 100 House and Senate subcommittees have jurisdiction over these programs. The generally haphazard development of federal programs in relation to each other and the difficulty in reorganizing programs imbedded in long-standing bureaucratic and political networks is part of the explanation for this phenomenon. A more important and fundamental explanation lies in the historical relationship between the federal government and postsecondary education. This relationship is defined by norms and basic assumptions that set out the limits of legitimate federal government action.

The strongest and most durable assumption of federal policy for post-secondary education is that public postsecondary education, and indeed all public education, is the primary responsibility of the states. At the Constitutional Convention of 1787, several proposed provisions of the new constitution were advanced to give the federal government the authority to establish institutions of higher education, or at least a national university as the "cap of the system." All of these proposals were rejected.[19] In fact, the word "education" does not appear in the Constitution. Thus we have not a national postsecondary education system but rather 50 state systems. The federal role in supporting postsecondary education has always been one of supplementing the states. Because the federal role has been to supplement state efforts, federal programs have aimed at specific federal purposes rather than at general support for education per se or the postsecondary education enterprise as a whole.

In addition, postsecondary education has generally been supported at all levels in the United States because it is "useful."[20] The national goals for which postsecondary education has been the useful means have changed over time: leadership training, public land development, manpower training for economic prosperity, scientific manpower for national defense, encouragement of citizen competence in self-government, promotion of international understanding, and most recently equal opportunity.[21]

The result of a federal role supplementing the basic state responsibility for postsecondary education and the view of postsecondary education as instrumental for the accomplishment of a wide range of federal goals has been fragmentation of federal efforts that impinge on postsecondary education. Postsecondary education programs are parcelled out among the agencies and subcommittees for whom they are a means to accomplish their particular goal, be it training military officers (Defense Department), promoting international understanding (State Department), or developing new sources of energy (Energy Research and Development Administration). Indeed, it would be seen as inappropriate by many for the federal government to have a single department of education or a comprehensive policy for postsecondary education since this would imply a derogation of the primary responsibility of the states in this area. Given this situation, there is no location in the congressional structure, or any strong inclination, to view federal efforts related to postsecondary education as a whole. Thus one consequence of the historical relationship between the federal government and postsecondary education is that policy making is never informed by a discussion of the full ramifications of a decision for postsecondary education or for other relevant federal programs. This obviously decreases the quality of congressional analysis of postsecondary education.

As the object of federal policy making, postsecondary education presents particular difficulties for researchers and data gatherers. Postsecondary education is an extremely diverse and pluralistic phenomenon. It includes two-year colleges, the traditional four-year collegiate institutions, research universities, proprietary schools, vocational-technical schools, religiously affiliated schools, secular institutions, colleges without walls, publics and privates. In addition, there is a great variety of relationships and affiliations of students and faculty to these institutions. There are more than 5,000 institutions enrolling more than 12 million students. It is simply technically difficult and extremely costly to gather systematic, reliable, and standardized information on even the most basic dimensions of postsecondary education for the guidance of policymakers.

In addition, postsecondary education in the United States, particularly in the collegiate and university sectors, is characterized by very strong traditions of institutional autonomy and academic freedom.[22] The recent cases of Hillsdale College and Brigham Young University challenging the right of the federal government to enforce sex discrimination guidelines are illustrative of the vitality of these traditions.[23] There is likewise a resistance to federally mandated data requirements. Institutions of postsecondary education have been skeptical of the unmitigated benevolence of the federal government and ever vigilant to resist federal intrusion, interference, or control. For example, a storm of protest greeted legislation proposed by the Department of Health, Education, and Welfare to provide consumer protection for students through tightening the standards for institutional eligibility for federal programs. A similar outcry greeted revised rules for monitoring payments of education benefits to veterans.[24] In both cases the heart of the controversy was federal interference with the academic prerogatives of postsecondary education institutions. One university representative characterized the veterans' benefits regulations as "another federal encroachment on institutional autonomy."[25] In these cases much of the attention focused on federal access to institutional records and federal prescription of statistical and recordkeeping requirements. Thus the traditions of academic freedom and institutional autonomy present another barrier to well-informed congressional decision making in the arena of postsecondary education policy making.

Many Different Worlds

A fundamental limit on the ability of congressmen to receive and use relevant information in the decision-making process is that the criteria applied by congressmen to determine what is relevant information and the criteria applied by those who supply information to Congress are different. Congress has an institutional perspective and institutional needs that produce data requirements that the data providers outside of Congress do not share because of their own institutional perspectives and needs. Congress, the executive branch, and the postsecondary education community lack *verstehen*—mutual understanding and empathy, the ability to put themselves in the other guy's shoes and anticipate his needs and constraints.

Analysts in the executive branch and postsecondary education are treated with substantial skepticism by congressmen and their staffs. In part, the suspicion is founded on the fact that the predictions and projections of analysts have turned out so frequently to be wrong. Large numbers of colleges have not closed their doors, not as many students as predicted have taken advantage of the basic grant, and the growth of state scholarship programs has far exceeded expectations.

More importantly, legislative policymakers and policy analysts in the executive branch and outside of government reach decisions on desirable courses of action in basically different ways. Analysts quite properly begin with questions, develop measures and analytic techniques to answer the questions, and finally produce the answers. The legislators, as politicians, are concerned above all with the answers, the results, the impact, who will get what—"the bottom line." To them, analysis is often perceived as an analytic trap. Implicit in most questions are values and preferences. These are often unintended and unknown even to the analyst. This is particularly true as the questions and analytic techniques become more abstract and are cast in terms of statistical procedures, models, and simulations. A legislator who buys into the apparently innocent and objective questions runs the risk of being locked into conclusions that are politically unacceptable. It is very difficult to disown "advice" that is solicited by a congressional source and bears the legitimacy of scientific inquiry.

Even if unbiased and objective questions were possible, legislators would still be wary of endorsing a scheme that leads to recommendations that are not knowable in advance. It is not that legislators have no interest in the facts or cannot be persuaded by rational arguments on the merits of the issues. But rather they want to consider issues by a dialectical process that relates the evidence and the policy implications. They want to constantly compare the data and the conclusions to which it leads in tandem. They are most leery of endorsing a system or process of analysis whose conclusions are not apparent. The 1973 report of the National Commission on the Financing of Postsecondary Education has had little apparent impact in the 1974-1976 review of the basic higher education legislation. An important reason for this is that the commission was charged with developing "alternative models for the long range solution to the problems of financing postsecondary education" and it carried out its task in large part by producing "an analytic framework."[26]

Abstract rationality quickly loses its relevance in the legislative world of political reality. For example, HR 3471, the Student Financial Aid Act of 1975, introduced by Congressman James O'Hara, chairman of the Subcommittee on Postsecondary Education, proposes extensive changes in the State Student Incentive Grant program. Among the most significant of the proposed changes is a new formula for allocating the funds among the states to match state student-aid grants. This complex formula is designed to measure a state's "effort" in supporting postsecondary education and to reward with federal dollars those states making the greatest relative effort. The O'Hara formula is based on the proposals of education policy analysts at the National Center for Higher Education Management Systems. While there might be a consensus on some of the general objectives of the formula, it has proven to be a source of embarrassment to O'Hara. A breakdown of the allocation of funds among the states by this formula indicated that one state, California, would receive 25 percent of the money. In its original form, the formula was therefore quickly dismissed as unacceptable and unrealistic by most other members of the Subcommittee. The legislators acted on the basis of the data and rejected the analytic system.

From their respective institutions, legislators, executive branch officials, and postsecondary educators often fail to communicate effectively with each other because each speaks the language of their specialized environment. A crucial dimension of the congressman's role is the enactment of laws. Laws are written in statutory language, presumably distinguished by its clarity and precision and utilizing the legal vocabulary that relates it to previous law and judicial opinions. Also historically over half the members of Congress have been lawyers.[27] As sculptors work in stone, legislators work in legislative language. In addition, however, legislators are popularly elected politicians, and they are accustomed to having explanations in the same popular vernacular that they would use at a PTA meeting, Kiwanis luncheon, or union hall. Congressmen work and communicate in legislative language and explain their efforts in everyday English. Members of Congress are also compelled to be generalists. Beyond the few specialists in each policy arena, most members do not understand the specialized jargon associated with all the issues they must pass on. The higher education specialists have only a vague notion of the meaning of a "Eurodollar," and the international trade experts are similarly adrift when confronted by a "cost of instruction allowance."

In contrast to the legislators, the executive branch officials speak in the uniquely convoluted style that is born of bureaucratic caution and complexity. They banter in acronyms: "The FIPSE proposal has to be reviewed by ASPE." The educators tend to speak in the eloquent rhetoric of the academy. They leave the legislators with a warm glow of high ideals but frequently without the words of legislative art that could transform noble sentiments into legislative realities. Alternatively, academics and bureaucrats speak in the tongue of education and social science research jargon, lacing their remarks with "multiple regressions," "cognitive constructs," "learning modules," and "synergy at the interfaces." Legislators, bureaucrats, and academics all communicate in language that is functional for daily interaction in their own environments. There are unfortunately too few effective translators when they come together, and legislators fail to use the information they receive because they often cannot understand it.

The worlds of the legislator, the bureaucrat, and the academic are also separated by different time horizons and styles that inhibit the flow of information to Congress. Congressmen have both a short- and a long-time perspective. The short-time horizon is a function of avoiding issues and keeping options open as long as possible. This is done to avoid taking politically damaging stands by making an early commitment and then having conditions or public opinion shift by the time the actual decision is made. In addition, given the crush of congressional business and responsibility, the attention of congressmen tends to become focused only as a deadline for action becomes imminent. When statutes expire, Congress is about to adjourn, or the election approaches (with numbing regularity every two years for House members), the legislators are galvanized into action. The typical pattern is a long period of drift as an issue is nurtured by a few members or the staff, followed by a period of frenetic activity as a deadline approaches and more members must get involved. This often produces a flood of requests for analysis and information on rather short notice. In contrast to this pattern, the bureaucracy moves with a carefully measured tread. The bureaucratic hierarchy that produces a single policy on behalf of the executive branch requires that requests for comment and recommendations must be circulated and cleared through many offices and levels before answers can be sent to Congress with an official imprimatur. Congenital bureaucratic prudence also slows the reaction time of the executive branch, with the result that responses to congressional requests are often not delivered in a timely fashion.

The postsecondary education community seems constrained to produce information that is not only responsive to congressional needs but that is also legitimate in academia. The result is careful and scholarly works that turn out to be handy as reference material but which arrive too late to be relevant in legislative decision making.

On the other hand, the time horizon of legislators is also long. Senators serve six-year terms and more than 90 percent of the members who seek reelection are successful.[28] Thus congressmen can view their efforts in terms of a career that often spans decades. For this reason as well as practical political constraints, legislators tend to view policy development in evolutionary and incremental rather than revolutionary and comprehensive terms.[29] Congressmen share this longer perspective with the permanent cadres of the executive branch. However, the President and his political appointees want to show results within their four-year term or at least within the eight years to which the Constitution limits a President's tenure. The academic community, confident of the truths it has discovered, lacking permanent involvement in politics, and naïve about the legislative process, is also frequently impatient with the pace of congressional action. When the political executive and educators are producing analyses and recommendations to accomplish things in a time frame significantly shorter than the legislators, they are once again talking past each other.

The basic attitudes and styles of the legislators, bureaucrats, and academics impede easy communication. Educators and legislative politicians frequently view each other with suspicion and misunderstanding. Speaking from long experience, Samuel Halperin argues that they have "two world views." The educators tend to view the legislators as unprincipled, overly pragmatic, unethical, tied to narrow interests, uninformed, and arrogant. From the other side, the legislators see the educators as sanctimonious, olympian, fuzzy, abstract, unappreciative of political reality and the legitimacy of the political process, and always demanding more while unwilling to be held accountable.[30] This mutual disregard often makes the relations between educators and legislators distant and uneasy. It inhibits informal contacts and easy access.

Similar stereotypes influence the views legislators and bureaucrats have of each other. But more importantly tension between these two sets of actors that inhibits the flow of information is inherent in the American system. The separation of powers and checks and balances are more than textbook cliches. They are realities of political life in Washington. There is a continual contest for institutional prerogative. Both branches want to make policy, the executive branch through dominance of legislative initiative and by maximizing administrative discretion in program operations and Congress through lawmaking and oversight of executive performance. The 1973 War Powers Act and the Congressional Budget and Impoundment Control Act of 1974 were major battles, but there are continually skirmishes between the two branches in each policy arena.

For example, during consideration of the Education Amendments of 1972, the issue of "educational renewal" arose. On the merits of the issue, the more effective delivery and coordination of federal elementary and secondary school programs, there was no real disagreement. It was instead fundamentally a contest over policy-making authority. Senate supporters of the amendment offered by Senator Cranston of California to prohibit HEW from pursuing educational renewal contended that it was a new "program" lacking legislative authorization. Executive branch opponents of the Cranston Amendment maintained that it was simply an administrative "strategy" and a proper exercise of administrative discretion. Congress won that round by a sweeping prohibition against the techniques HEW had used to justify educational renewal. But the war goes on, as the Founding Fathers intended, and it is yet another barrier to the smooth flow of information from the executive branch to the Congress. Information is not only to be shared for the attainment of mutually agreed on public goals; it is also a valuable resource in the contest for power between the two branches.

For the last eight years the inherent conflict between the two branches has been exacerbated by the division in party control of Congress and the presidency. The majority party congressional Democrats mistrust information from the executive branch both because it is from the *executive* branch and because it is from the *Republican* executive branch. There is also a reticence to solicit information from the executive branch both because "those are not our guys over there" and because the questions asked as one develops a legislative initiative could easily tip off one's partisan opponents in the executive branch. Partisan legislative-executive tension reached its zenith during President Nixon's second term when legislative proposals as a strategy for shaping policy were largely abandoned in favor of controlling policy through regulation, impounding, executive reorganization, and the budget.[31]

Not a partisan but an ideological schism may be developing between the higher education community and the legislators with the primary responsibility for postsecondary education programs. The associations that are the voice of postsecondary education in Washington represent institutions. Their constituency is college and university presidents and other administrators—postsecondary education's *management*. By a decision of the National Labor Relations Board in 1970, the employees of private colleges and universities were accorded federal collective bargaining rights.[32] In recent years legislation to bring the employees of state and local governments, including those at public postsecondary institutions, under federal jurisdiction, has been under consideration in Congress. The management of postsecondary education and their Washington spokesmen have been generally unsympathetic and opposed to the growth of collective bargaining on the campuses. The House Education and Labor Committee and the Senate Labor and Public Welfare Committee have jurisdiction over the collective bargaining legislation. Both committees also have a heavy predominance of prolabor liberals who favor the expansion of collective bargaining. These same committees have jurisdiction over much of the legislation affecting postsecondary education. As the Washington spokesmen for postsecondary education find themselves on the antilabor and antiunion side of the collective bargaining issue, they may also find that the sympathy with which their problems have been heard on education issues will decline. This would add a new hurdle in the way of effective communication of ideas and information between the postsecondary education community and Congress.

Finally, the institutional perspectives of bureaucrats and educators lead them to gather data and to organize it in formats that do not necessarily match the needs of congressmen. Educators are primarily concerned with the internal management of their institutions, and the bureaucrats are most interested in overall program impact and performance. Neither of them routinely organizes data, for example, by state or congressional district, which is a dimension of preeminent concern to most elected representatives.

Weakness of the Information Sources

The U.S. Office of Education and the institutions and associations in postsecondary education are the primary providers of information to Congress for postsecondary education policy making. These institutions suffer from weaknesses that limit their ability to effectively serve the information needs of the legislature.

Overload is the critical problem at the Office of Education. Created in 1867, the Office of Education was for almost 100 years a quiet federal backwater devoted largely to a limited role in the collection and dissemination of educational statistics and to technical consultation.[33] Even this limited role was focused almost exclusively on elementary and secondary schooling to the exclusion of postsecondary education. Beginning as a steady stream in the 1950s and growing to a torrent in the 1960s, the Office of Education was deluged with new programs and responsibilities. An old-line bureau, low in prestige, understaffed, with archaic management practices, and a service orientation was suddenly asked to undertake major responsibilities for program operations on the cutting edge of a new domestic agenda. These responsibilities were not only in the somewhat familiar elementary and secondary field but also in the unfamiliar realm of postsecondary education. This was done in the context of the trauma of frequent reorganizations, rapid turnover of commissioners and other personnel, and a continuing succession of new programs and amendments to old programs passed by Congress.[34] The Office of Education has been playing catch-up for more than a decade, and it has not yet caught up. The Office of Education is also obviously constrained by the complexity of postsecondary education and the resistance to federal "meddling."

Basic data on student-assistance programs are usually at least two years old when published by the Office of Education. Recent testimony before the Senate Permanent Subcommittee on Investigations revealed deplorable misman-agement in the federal guaranteed student loan programs that have an annual volume of more than $4 billion. The Office of Education was not effectively gathering even the most rudimentary information necessary for monitoring and evaluating the programs.[35] In many cases, Congress lacks the information it needs for good decision making because the Office of Education is incapable of supplying it.

In the case of the postsecondary education community, the suspicion of politicians, traditions of academic freedom and institutional autonomy, diversity of postsecondary education and its unique language, style, time horizons, and basic data needs have all been mentioned as limits on the ability of institutions and their spokesmen to transmit, and Congress to get, information relevant to policy making. In addition, postsecondary education also suffers from relatively primitive management. While postsecondary education has advanced beyond quill pens and green eye shades, until quite recently management was largely disdained as beneath the concern of academics and scholars. Presidents and deans were chosen for their academic distinction, fund-raising ability, and political skill in dealing with students, faculty, alumni, and government officials, rather than their administrative skill or experience. Faced with fiscal stringency and government pressure for accountability, there is a management revolution underway in postsecondary education. But until the effects of this revolution have permeated more broadly and become institutionalized, the postsecondary education community will be in many ways incapable of telling Congress about itself, even if it wanted to.

Congress does not receive the information it needs and does not use what it receives effectively in decision making for a variety of diverse reasons. Many of these reasons go to the very nature of Congress, the executive branch, and postsecondary education and to their historical relationship in this country. The problem extends far beyond normal human frailty and cannot be resolved by any simple panacea. To search for "an answer" to the problem is to miss its true dimensions. The problem can be ameliorated on several fronts, but probably never "solved."

Comments

Samuel Halperin

Wolanin writes perceptively from the cockpit of one of the nation's principal centers for policy making in postsecondary education. On and off since 1971, as legislative assistant to a senior education representative and now as staff director of a key House subcommittee, he has "schemed and plotted with the best of them" to construct major legislation, including the far-reaching Education Amendments of 1972, responses to antibusing amendments, new initiatives in the arts and humanities, etc.

While his analysis is difficult to fault for those familiar with the environment in which Wolanin works and of which he writes, I would caution readers against too quickly assuming that all policy making in the Congress is as depicted here. The reasons for exercising such caution are at least three in number.

First, education policy in the Congress has been strongly dominated by a progressive Democratic liberal Republican consensus which holds that, in the field of education, "more is better" and which, virtually each year, enacts new cornucopias of educational largesse. Such is not the case in other substantive areas, e.g., energy, labor-management relations, or housing, where every bill is bitterly contested and where legislative output is measured not in pipelines but in eyedroppers.

Beginning in 1961, when Adam Clayton Powell assumed the chairmanship of the House Committee on Education and Labor and his leadership made that committee a force for passing, not stopping, education-aid bills, the bulk of the Congress has gradually become, at least nominally and for purposes of recorded votes, proeducation. Prodded successfully by Lyndon B. Johnson to do more for education, the House committee, under the unflagging leadership of Carl Perkins, and its even more eager Senate counterpart, the Committee on Labor and Public Welfare (led variously by such strong friends of education as Wayne Morse, Ralph Yarborough, Harrison Williams, and Claiborne Pell) have responded with "Christmas trees" of authorizing goodies for the nation's schools and colleges.

More to the point of this article, the members of these committees have developed an ethos that calls on them "to legislate." (In the words of one member: "My people elected me to make laws. If they had wanted otherwise, they could have elected a policeman or an accountant.") Divided though they may be on other issues, the dominant world view of members of the education subcommittees is to produce new authorizations for federal spending and related activity, either as free-standing public laws or, if need be, as part of massive and complex omnibus bills.

Thus in recent years the Education Amendments of 1972, when considered in conference committee, ran 754 pages in length while the 1974 omnibus bill totalled a mere 463 pages. Ask how many new programs or specific funds were authorized by such public laws, and the answer will vary with the observer; "At least 65 separate programs" in the Education Amendments of 1972 alone is the answer given by the House Committee on Education and Labor. While the exact numbers are debatable, everyone agrees that Congress's output of education programs has been prodigious. In postsecondary education alone, according to a Library of Congress survey, there are 439 separate programs or authorities.[36]

With a political culture stressing output and quantity, it is understandable that a "friendly competitiveness" characterizes the members and staffs of the three House education subcommittees as each vies to report out legislation in its areas of jurisdiction. The unwritten rule seems to be: Each subcommittee is entitled to report out one or more major bills each year. If the elementary-secondary education subcommittee gets a bill out, then the postsecondary subcommittee has its "turn." Everybody wins; nobody loses. Furthermore, when the House Committee on Education and Labor reports an education bill to the floor of the House of Representatives, it passes, usually overwhelmingly, and generally becomes the law of the land.

If the foregoing is a fair representation of the political culture in the congressional education committees, the implications of this culture for the use and misuse of information deserve further exploration, a task I shall partially undertake here. The point to be made here is that Dr. Wolanin's analysis is relevant to a particular political culture, not necessarily to the broader context of the Congress and information generally.

A second reason for resisting automatic acceptance of Dr. Wolanin's apt contribution as an accurate representation of how Congress as a whole deals with information relates closely to the first observation. In education, the stakes in federal policy making, other than personal-political, are relatively small. Often they are only marginal to the central concerns, curricula, and finances[37] of American schools and colleges that are overwhelmingly nonfederal in character. Associations and proeducation members lobby for what are useful but, nonetheless, small increments to existing programs or else for new starts at only modest funding levels.

But outside education, the legislative stakes are often multibillion dollar in character, affecting entire industries with immediate life-and-death consequences. The level of contention, with attendant Madison Avenue public relations campaigns, high-priced law firms, and similar apparatus, makes education politics seem "small potatoes." One former House Committee on Education and Labor member, now a midsenior member of the powerful Ways and Means Committee, exclaimed:

Those guys on Education and Labor don't know what pressure is. The education lobbyists are nice guys, dull but nice. Who gets excited about a phony authorization of $100 million for vocational education which we all know won't be appropriated in full and is unlikely to add more than 30 cents per kid even if funded? But when we [on Ways and Means] deal with oil or real estate, we half fear for our lives and families. The game we play here isn't marbles, but it's nevertheless played for keeps.

Finally, teachers and analysts alike must remember that authorization politics differ significantly from appropriations politics. As Richard Fenno and other students of the politics of the purse have chronicled, legislative committees

grant "hunting licenses" to interested parties in the form of program authorizations. Such committees are often under no real disciplinary constraints to limit
the dispensation of such hunting licenses. Appropriations committees, on the
other hand, dispense "real dollars" of which there are never enough to go
around. Members of the money committees know in advance, and take pride in
the fact, that they "can't please everybody" . . . and they don't try. They see
themselves as "tough," while they view their colleagues on authorizations as
"soft," particularly those who serve on "the do-gooder liberal committees like
Education and Labor." Appropriations members like to say that they give
dollars only to "proven" programs while they accuse their counterparts on
authorizing committees of "ignoring the facts," of "trying to please everybody,"
of never terminating "bad programs," and of generally creating false and
unreasonable expectations about what can, in fact, be funded.

In sum, the implications of these differing kinds of political cultures for the
use of information must be recognized. The reader should remember always the
specific context of Wolanin's analysis, thus insulating against overhasty generalization. What is true for education legislative decision making may well not apply
in other substantive areas, nor in the politics of the appropriations process.

Despite these important limitations of subject matter and process that
preclude regarding this work as a definitive statement of how the Congress as a
whole deals with information, I would also stress the many merits of Wolanin's
contribution. In particular, his chapter shows the richness and complexity with
which one must approach answers to so bold a question as "Why does legislative
policy making in education seem so 'irrational and haphazard'?" As Wolanin
skillfully shows, the answers are many, compounded of differences in values,
institutions, processes, constituencies, and even "language."

While I agree with most of his analysis, I would cavil in the following
respects: It is too sweeping and uncritical a generalization to say that "congressmen are asking the right questions" which are needed for making "substantively
good decisions." As I will argue below, members may ask "good" questions
when their minds are not made up, when they are not driving toward a
predetermined goal. However, since I believe that most members of the
education committees are truly "open" only a fraction of the time, I find motive
and direction, rather than an abstract searching for truth and certainty, behind
most members' questions. To Wolanin's dictum, "To get good data you have to
ask good questions," I would add: "And to get better policy you have to be
willing to receive the answers, regardless of where they might lead the questioner
in policy conclusions." This I don't believe most members are ready to do, most
of the time.

While all the factors cited by Wolanin as militating against either the receipt
of useful data or the incorporation of such data into the decision-making process
seem operative at least some of the time, Wolanin would have performed an even
more distinctive service if he had tried to isolate which one or two of several

dozen "diverse reasons" were *most* responsible for Congress not receiving or not using effectively the information it gets to make better decisions. Admittedly, there may not be "an answer." Yet, I shall argue, some of the factors seem far more "responsible" than others for this shortfall between information and policy.

Specifically, I believe that decision making in the education committees of the Congress is characterized primarily by a strong propensity to legislate new and expanded authorizations. The basic criteria determining what shall be legislated are whether a member (often but not always at the instigation of an activist staff aide) *believes* that something is "a good idea," whether that "good idea" can be made "politically salable," and whether potentially debilitating opposition can be removed.

Members believe that they are elected to legislate after they determine "what's needed." Pressures from educational interest groups are decidedly secondary to the members' own senses of "what's needed." Once this determination has been made—usually by a simple statement of the problem, evidence of "unmet need," and, seldom, by discovery of proven models for effectively addressing the problem—the member organizes his or her own "effective demand" for the legislation by seeking out fellow members and associations, prestigious individuals, and occasionally allies within the executive branch. In all these acts of policy formulation and coalition building, the role of information is consistently instrumental to the preconceived goal that is, in Representative Perkins's telling phrase: "We're gonna get a bill."

Thus the interest of most members in the committees in question is to pass legislation. Qualitative improvements in the process that do not truly address the "interests" (in the Madisonian sense) of the members themselves, the prime movers in this social subsystem, have little chance of adoption. For any reform to be effective, for example, for information to be used better, it must first appeal to the members and their preeminent desire to author new statutes or to defend old programs that are perceived as serving their value preferences, constituency interests, and personal legislative "track records." (Note that the majority of the House Committee on Education and Labor has served on that committee since the late fifties and early sixties. While Presidents, HEW secretaries, and U.S. commissioners of education have come and gone in great profusion, these members continue to pass judgment on the same landmark statutes that they originally authored in 1958, 1963, 1965, 1968, 1972, 1974, etc.)

In short, most of the time, members (and their staffs) are not in abstract search of better information on which to base a policy to be formulated at some indefinite point in the future. Rather, the member "knows" in advance that he supports programs that, for example, channel funds into cities rather than rural areas, or programs that help poor nonwhites disproportionately to the middle class, or programs that help students first and institutions only secondarily, and so forth. The member seeks information to promote such interests or to contend against perceived threats to those interests, regardless of the source of those threats.

Therefore, it comes as no great surprise to note how in recent years a liberal and activist education Congress has resisted with relative ease both the "tainted evaluative studies" presented by the Nixon-Ford Administration and by "those misanthropic academics" whom Congress views alike as "antieducation," as "antipeople." Even critical reports from Congress's own General Accounting Office get short shrift if they tend to question the efficacy of a given program; exposing executive branch maladministration, is, on the other hand, always "fair game" (and has been since the first presidency).

In short, information in the congressional education setting is seldom sought for its own sake or as an aid to policy making in general. It serves a generally preconceived point of view. If it advances a given commitment, data are trumpeted over and over again. Contrariwise, "harmful" data are not wanted and are quickly ignored. Ultimately, observes Wolanin, what members most rely on is not information but "their judgment and their values." And this is true whether information exists or does not!

Thus all schemes for improving the utilization of information depend ultimately on their appeal to the predominant interests of members. It will do little good, given the present predilections of the majority of education committee members, to argue for structural and procedural changes (e.g., fewer subcommittees, permanent authorizations for "successful" programs, better policy analysis services, etc.) unless one can relate such changes to the prevailing value preferences of the members. Those innovations have the best chance of being adopted by the Congress that seem to promise "more for education" and that do not challenge the prevailing value commitments of the present committees. Reform must be based on incentives, not merely on merit.

As an example, the reason that the Developing Institutions program—Title III of the Higher Education Act of 1965—has never had a thorough airing is not *primarily* because of congressional preoccupation with other, more volatile issues. Rather, it is a fairly deeply held conviction on the part of the relative handful of members who make education policy that Title III funds are going to the "right" institutions—black colleges, community colleges, small but promising colleges. The fact that even the notoriously "antieducation" Nixon-Ford Administration increased budgets for this program from $30 million in fiscal 1969 to $110 million in fiscal 1976 is almost "enough information" in and of itself to deepen the congressional conviction that "Title III must be OK if those SOBs in the Administration aren't trying to cut it."

The foregoing point of view (one hesitates to call so straightforward an account of congressional behavior an "analysis"!) must not be construed as an allegation that Congress is biased or that "facts do not count" or that "information is useless." To the contrary, members of Congress are highly skilled professionals, intelligent, and substantially above average, disposed toward "solving problems and helping people." Information that is cogent and concise, that is expressed in dejargonized terms, and that is stated compellingly in its claim to a hearing, *will* tend to have an impact. Let academics beware, however, of assuming that "the facts" dictate outcomes. The seedbed of values and judgments of our elected representatives must first be prepared before the seeds of information may truly germinate. And that, I take it, is what the democratic process is, and should be, all about.

Notes

1. Fred Schwengel, "Information Handling: 'For a Vast Future Also,' " in *We Propose: A Modern Congress*, ed. Mary McInnis (New York: McGraw-Hill, 1966), p. 303.

2. "Organization of the Congress," *Report of the Joint Committee on the Organization of Congress* (LaFollette-Monroney Committee Report), Senate Report 1011, 79th Cong., 2d sess., pp. 9-11, 14-18; "Committee Reform Amendments of 1974," *Report of the Select Committee on Committees* (Bolling Committee Report), House Report 93-916, Part II, pp. 19, 20, 72-74; Schwengel, "Information Handling"; Charles L. Clapp, *The Congressman: His Work as He Sees It* (Garden City, N.Y.: Doubleday, 1963), pp. 476-77; Mark J. Green, James M. Fallows, and David R. Zwick, *Who Runs Congress?* (New York: Bantam Books, 1972), pp. 101-107; Committee for Economic Development, *Making Congress More Effective* (New York: Committee for Economic Development, 1970), pp. 50-51; Committee for Economic Development, *Congressional Decision Making for National Security* (New York: Committee for Economic Development, 1974), pp. 38-48; and Roger H. Davidson, David M. Kovenock, and Michael K. O'Leary, *Congress in Crisis: Politics and Congressional Reform* (Belmont, Calif.: Wadsworth, 1966), p. 175.

3. *Congressional Record*, daily ed., July 29, 1975, p. S 14129.

4. Ibid., p. S 14128.

5. *New York Times*, December 28, 1975, p. 26.

6. Harold Jenkins, "Legislative-Executive Disagreement: Interpreting the 1972 Amendments to the Guaranteed Student Loan Program," *Harvard Journal on Legislation* 10 (April 1973): 485.

7. These questions and those in the following paragraphs are paraphrases of actual questions asked in longer and less direct form in recent hearings.

8. The question of the measurement and existence of student financial need is treated in detail, for example, in "Student Financial Assistance (Theory and Practice of Needs Analysis)," *Hearings before the House Special Subcommittee on Education*, 93rd Cong., 1st sess., Part I.

9. On the limits of social analysis, see Alice M. Rivlin, *Systematic Thinking for Social Action* (Washington, D.C.: The Brookings Institution, 1971), chap. 5; Isaiah Berlin, *The Hedgehog and the Fox* (New York: Simon and Schuster, 1966), pp. 31, 68; and Charles E. Lindblom, *The Policy-making Process* (Englewood Cliffs, N.J.: Prentice-Hall, 1968), pp. 14-15.

10. On nonverifiable values, see Lindblom, *The Policy-making Process*, pp. 16-17; and Herbert A. Simon, *Administrative Behavior*, 2d ed. (New York: Free Press, 1965), pp. 45-60.

11. This point is amply demonstrated in the variety of "Day in the Life of the Congressman" articles [for example, James Boyd, "What Happens to a Senator's Day," *The Washington Monthly* (February 1969)] or in the unanimous testimony in the statements of members announcing their retirement (for example, " 'Mosher's Law'—Better to Retire Too Early Than Too Late," *Congressional Record*, daily ed., December 12, 1975, pp. E 6669-6671).

12. Quoted in George Goodwin, Jr., *The Little Legislatures: Committees of Congress* (Amherst, Mass.: University of Massachusetts Press, 1970), p. 46.

13. This would be a decision-making process analogous to that suggested by Amitai Etzioni in "Mixed-Scanning: A 'Third' Approach to Decision-Making," *Public Administration Review* (Dec. 1967).

14. Irving Janis, *Victims of Groupthink* (Boston: Houghton Mifflin, 1972).

15. *Congressional Record*, daily ed., December 13, 1974, pp. S 21486-S 21491.

16. See Nelson Polsby, "Policy Analysis and Congress," *Public Policy* 18 (Fall 1969): 69. We certainly do not advocate that Congress become more hierarchical and bureaucratic or even necessarily imply that the lack of efficiency and rationality in congressional information processing is a severe congressional defect. The effective injection of political representation into public policy decisions is perhaps the central role of the Congress.

17. "Higher Education Amendments of 1971," *Hearings before House Special Subcommittee on Education*, 92nd Cong., 1st sess. (1971), pp. 773-783.

18. The National Commission on the Financing of Postsecondary Education, *Financing Postsecondary Education in the United States* (Washington, D.C.: Government Printing Office, 1973), p. 106.

19. George N. Rainsford, *Congress and Higher Education in the Nineteenth Century* (Knoxville, Tenn.: University of Tennessee Press, 1972), p. 17.

20. See Oscar Handlin and Mary Handlin, *The American College and American Culture* (New York: McGraw-Hill, 1970), p. 2.

21. These and other basic assumptions of federal policy making for postsecondary education are analyzed in greater detail in Thomas Wolanin and Lawrence Gladieux, "The Political Culture of a Policy Arena: Higher Education," in *What Government Does*, eds. Matthew Holden, Jr., and Dennis Dresang (Beverly Hills, Calif.: Sage Publications, 1975).

22. Joseph Ben-David, *American Higher Education: Directions Old and New* (New York: McGraw-Hill, 1972), pp. 11-23.

23. See *Chronicle of Higher Education*, Oct. 28, 1975, pp. 1, 10 and Nov. 3, 1975, pp. 5, 6.

24. *Chronicle of Higher Education*, December 15, 1975, pp. 1, 6, 9.

25. Quoted in *Chronicle of Higher Education*, p. 9.

26. The National Commission on the Financing of Postsecondary Education, *Financing Postsecondary Education*, pp. 5-8.

27. Malcolm E. Jewell and Samuel C. Patterson, *The Legislative Process in the United States*, 2d ed. (New York: Random House, 1973), pp. 73-77.

28. William Keefe and Morris S. Ogul, *The American Legislative Process: Congress and the States*, 3rd ed. (Englewood Cliffs, N.J.: Prentice-Hall, 1973), p. 109.

29. See, for example, Richard Fenno, *The Power of the Purse: Appropriations Politics in Congress* (Boston: Little, Brown, 1966), *passim.*

30. Samuel Halperin, "Politicians and Educators: Two World Views," *Phi Delta Kappan* (November 1974).

31. See Richard P. Nathan, *The Plot That Failed: Nixon and the Administrative Presidency* (New York: Wiley, 1975), chap. 4.

32. *Cornell University*, 183 NLRB No. 41 (1970).

33. Stephen K. Bailey and Edith K. Mosher, *ESEA: The Office of Education Administers a Law* (Syracuse, N.Y.: Syracuse University Press, 1968), p. 17.

34. Stephen K. Bailey and Edith K. Mosher, *ESEA: The Office of Education Administers a Law* (Syracuse, N.Y.: Syracuse University Press, 1968), chap. 3.

35. See "Federal Student Loan Program in Deep Trouble," *Congressional Record*, daily ed., Nov. 17, 1975, pp. S 20175-S 20182.

36. Interestingly enough, only 117 of these programs are under the jurisdiction of the House Committee on Education and Labor. See R.C. Andringa, "The View from the Hill," *Change* 8 (April 1976): 26-29.

37. In elementary-secondary education, for example, federal funds comprise only about 7 percent of all expenditures and, in real purchasing power, have been shrinking as a fraction of all spending.

5 John Rawls and Educational Policy

Tyll van Geel

John Rawls, professor of philosophy at Harvard University, is one of the major social philosophers of this century, and his book *A Theory of Justice* is one of the major works of social philosophy of most any century.[1] Since its publication in 1971, the book has evoked widespread comment both in praise and criticism, and one cannot doubt that social philosophy from this point forward will have to contend with what Rawls has said.

Beyond the undoubted impact Rawls will have on social philosophy, his work has implications for social policy itself, most importantly on such issues as liberty and the acquisition, transfer, and distribution of material goods, income, and wealth. But while the book concentrates on these issues, Rawls does address himself to education, and with further analysis we can extract from his work a virtually complete philosophy of education with important policy implications.

This essay begins with a brief summary of what appears to be the current dominant social philosophical position on education in the United States as a way of providing a background against which to discuss Rawls's theory. A brief introduction to Rawls's methodology and mode of argument then follows as a way of establishing the premises necessary for an understanding of Rawls's principles and his philosophy of education. Next Rawls's principles are discussed in a general way with a view to their implications for education. A concluding section attempts to probe beneath the surface of Rawls's writing to extract a more complete understanding of the implications of *A Theory of Justice* for educational policy.

A warning: This essay does not attempt to provide a criticism of the premises, the methodology, or the logic Rawls employed—all of which have been criticized in print—but is instead an interpretative essay designed to flesh out the meaning and implications of *A Theory of Justice*. However, the more we understand what Rawls is saying, the more we will be in a position to decide if we accept his theory and the resulting policy implications.

Current Realities

Rawls develops three concepts that he terms "perfect, imperfect, and pure procedural justice," terms that are extremely useful not only in obtaining a full grasp of his philosophical system but also in perceiving the current moral code that seems to be the basic underpinning for educational policy in the United

121

States. Perfect procedural justice obtains when there is an independent criterion for determining the acceptability of an outcome of a process and there exists a process that is sure to achieve the desired outcome. For example, if a cake is to be divided equally (the independent criterion) among self-interested people, a procedure sure to achieve this result is to make the person who cuts the cake choose the last piece. Imperfect procedural justice is illustrated by the criminal trial. The desired outcome is that only the guilty are convicted, but there is no procedure that can be established to assure such a result in all cases. And pure procedural justice obtains when there is no independent criterion for the right result, as for example, with a game of chance. There, whatever the distribution of winnings and losses, the result must be deemed fair if the procedure was fair and fairly carried out.

Our current political-economic-social system can be conceived as a system of imperfect procedural justice with the independent criterion being the greatest good for the greatest number. A basic principle for guiding the establishment of institutions and policies designed to realize this criterion is that of equal opportunity which means that people of equal ability and motivation should have equal chances in achieving their personal life plans. Fair access to those opportunity, which means that people of equal ability and motivation should problem since some children are born to parents who neglect their education and others are born to parents who lack monetary and other capacities to provide the needed education. Hence states have adopted compulsory education and neglect laws to take care of the problem of neglect and have supported the creation of public systems of education in order to provide all children with an equal educational opportunity. Thus children have been given the opportunity to obtain emotional nurture, guidance, training, and education in the family as well as the opportunity to obtain similar services in public institutions. In providing these public services the guiding principle has been that children should be provided with merely equal services and facilities but that they would not be assured that these services actually meet their particular and individual educational needs. The stress has been on equal *opportunities*, not equal results.

Historically our effort to provide equal opportunity has been imperfect in several respects. Children who through luck were born into families with the will and capacity to provide strong educational support benefit doubly—in their homes and in the public schools. On the basis of their race alone millions of students have been provided public educational opportunities inferior to the opportunities afforded students of other races. As for the amount of money to be spent on the children in the public schools, legislatures have arranged matters so that the level of spending is a function of local school district property wealth, local district income, and local district political will.[2] As a consequence there are vast disparities in the educational opportunities afforded children. Indeed, some children are afforded no publicly supported educational opportunities whatsoever, namely, those millions of mentally retarded children who are permissibly excluded from the public schools, not to speak of the millions of students that public officials and parents let languish on the streets or who are deliberately pushed out of schools once they are beyond the age of compulsory attendance.[3] Those students who remain are grouped and tracked in such a way that those relegated to the lower tracks are given a watered down education largely designed to funnel them into blue-collar jobs.[4] And millions of non-English-speaking students are provided an all-English educational program from which they derive no benefits.[5]

Obviously if the equal-opportunity strategy was going to work and to continue to be accepted as the basic social policy approach in the country, reform of the educational system was necessary. As a consequence, attempts have been made to make more equal the opportunities afforded by the public schools, but whether one talks of racial segregation, reform of educational finance systems, the exclusion of children from school, tracking, or the functional exclusion of the non-English speaking, these reform efforts are hardly near completion. Meanwhile research has shown that the schools have failed in the task of assuring all children regardless of their social class background of an equal opportunity in the race for those rewards the century may offer. There remains a strong correlation between educational failure, on the one hand, and, on the other hand, race and low social class background.[6]

The slowness in the reform of the educational system is but one factor in a turning away from heavy reliance on the mechanism of equal opportunity. Daniel Bell notes five other points in the case against equal opportunity.[7] First, if the concept actually worked so that those with greater ability did reap more rewards, we would then be distributing the goods of our society on the basis of abilities the successful individuals did not earn but simply obtained through luck in the genetic lottery. Modern moral intuition asserts that having won out in nature's game of chance is hardly a moral basis for obtaining a larger share of the socially produced product. Second, high-status parents usually have been able to pass on advantages to their offspring either by purchasing extra educational services for their children or by providing that education themselves, let alone using influence to obtain jobs and positions for their children. Third, it appears that luck as much as anything else accounts for the ultimate social status that people achieve.[8] Fourth, the competitive system fostered by the notion of equal opportunity has among its effects the stigmatization of those who do less well, even if the determinants of this lower status were beyond the individual's personal control. Fifth, the whole system seems to allow for great inequalities in the distribution of wealth, and those groups that have "made it" can legitimately insist on using principles of merit they know have the effect of precluding low-status groups from gaining access to jobs and other rewards. And we might add to Bell's list the belief that schools—except perhaps at extraordinary expense—cannot be made to compensate for the unequal starts children get from their unequal families.

These problems with implementing a system of equal opportunity have led to new developments in social philosophy. Some social theorists argue that what is needed is not an abandonment of the notion of equal opportunity but special steps to mitigate the failings of the system such as the establishment of a variety of income-maintenance programs like social security, welfare, and food and housing programs. Those who argue for these programs also seem to be moving toward a new independent criterion for assessing social-economic outcomes. The suggested criteria include assuring that basic needs are met if and when they arise; maximizing the income of the lowest income groups; maximizing average income per person; and/or reducing the existing relative inequalities in income. One of those arguing for a new social philosophy is John Rawls, who in his *A Theory of Justice* establishes one of the most comprehensive social philosophical systems ever written.

Rawls's Method and Argument

Rawls can be understood as beginning his work with a particular moral and psychological conception of people:

Moral persons are distinguished by two features: first they are capable of having (and are assumed to have) a conception of their good (as expressed by a rational plan of life); and second they are capable of having (and are assumed to acquire) a sense of justice, a normally effective desire to apply and to act upon the principles of justice at least to a minimum degree (p. 505).

Rawls also assumes that moral persons are entitled to equal justice. The assumption of a right to equal justice leads Rawls to say that moral persons have an equal right to participate in the formulation of the principles and other institutions that are to govern their cooperative activities (pp. 221-222, 478).

As already suggested by the definition of a moral person, the good of a person is determined by what is for him the most rational plan of life (p. 395). Of course, what is rational for one person may not be for another. All that Rawls suggests is that certain almost commonsensical principles are to be followed in developing a rational plan, the ends of which are for the individual to decide on consistent with the principles of justice yet to be specified (p. 407 ff).

At this point Rawls introduces several other assumptions. First, he posits that the kinds of plans people will develop for themselves will be influenced by what he calls the "Aristotelian Principle." This principle provides that "other things being equal, human beings enjoy the exercise of their realized capacities (their innate or trained abilities), and this enjoyment increases the more the capacity is realized, or the greater its complexity" (p. 426). He then adds:

The intuitive idea here is that human beings take more pleasure in doing something as they become more proficient at it, and of two activities they do equally well, they prefer the one calling on a larger repertoire of more intricate and subtle discriminations. For example, chess is a more complicated and subtle game than checkers, and algebra is more intricate than elementary arithmetic. Thus the principle says that someone who can do both generally prefers playing chess to playing checkers, and that he would rather study algebra than arithmetic (p. 426).

This principle leads people to develop more complex and comprehensive life plans (pp. 414, 427, 428). Further, Rawls says the principle characterizes human beings as being importantly moved not only by the pressure of bodily needs but also by the desire to do things enjoyed simply for their own sakes at least after urgent and pressing wants are satisfied (p. 431). Further, having a life plan that satisfies the Aristotelian Principle is one of the prerequisites for enjoying self-respect (p. 440). (Self-respect is defined as having two aspects: (1) a person's sense of his own value, his secure conviction that his conception of his good, his plan of life, is worth carrying out, and (2) self-respect implies a confidence in one's ability, so far as it is within one's power, to fulfill one's intentions (p. 440).) And having a sense of self-respect is no small matter since Rawls says that "without it [self-respect] nothing may seem worth doing, or if some things have value for us, we lack the will to strive for them. All desire and activity becomes empty and vain, and we sink into apathy and cynicism" (p. 440).

With these assumptions in mind Rawls turns to the concept of "primary goods," the theory of which he admits "depends on psychological premises and these may prove incorrect" (p. 260, and see 432). The concept of primary goods is the notion that there are certain things that are useful means to a wide range of ends; these goods anybody would want regardless of what rational life plan he adopts (p. 62). Rawls's list includes wealth and power, rights and liberties, opportunities and powers, and a sense of one's own worth (p. 92). Because of the Aristotelian Principle, Rawls cannot only specify these primary goods but can also suggest which are the most important to people. The most important among the primary goods are liberty, opportunities, and self-worth.

Rawls makes one other assumption about people that does not logically follow from what has been said but which is consistent with the previous assumptions. He assumes people are "mutually disinterested," meaning they are neither so benevolent as to be primarily concerned with helping one another, nor so envious that they cannot tolerate differences, inequalities, between themselves (pp. 129, 143).

In the next step Rawls asks the question, what sort of principles of justice would free, equal, and rational people with the psychological characteristics described above choose for regulating their society? He answers the question by running a mental experiment in which he imagines that people like he just described are in a situation he calls the "original position" where they are given the task of choosing a set of principles for regulating their society (p. 11). Rawls imposes special conditions on his people as they work through their problem: They are to work under a "veil of ignorance," meaning they know nothing specific about their society or about themselves (pp. 12, 136 ff). All they know are general things such as that their society is economically at least moderately well-off and they are rational beings who in that society will have different life plans and places in the society. They do not know what their own talents, abilities, plans, or status in the society actually will be. Rawls says the effect of the veil of ignorance is that no one is able to bargain for principles of justice that favor his particular condition (p. 12). Further, since all share in the same set of facts, they are led to reason from the same premises. This fact, Rawls says, means that voting can be on the basis of unanimity (p. 564). Each person is in essence given a veto, thus each is assured he has an equal right with others to participate in choosing the principles of justice.

Rawls says the procedure of the original position is an example of pure procedural justice (p. 120). He also says that this procedure reflects the "moral point of view" or is a way of modeling the moral point of view we use when thinking about moral problems such as selecting principles of justice (pp. 21-22, 518). The procedure is a way of demonstrating what principles autonomous, equal, free, and rational people would choose to impose on themselves (p. 251 ff).

Rawls then describes the mental calculations of the people in the original position as they work toward an agreement on a set of principles. Rawls says his people would select a set of principles the consequences of which they know they could live with once the veil of ignorance is lifted. "They are rational in that they will not enter into agreements they know they cannot keep, or can do so only with great difficulty" (p. 145). The kind of agreement they could live with, of course, is importantly dependent on their psychological characteristics, a point the importance of which will become evident momentarily.

Next Rawls sets out to establish that it would be rational for these people to go about their task *as if* they had an aversion to risk (the parties because of the veil of ignorance do not in fact know this aspect of their personal psychologies) (p. 172). Put differently, Rawls wants to establish that it is rational for the parties to choose among the principles of justice in light of the maximin decision rule that holds that they are to adopt the principles the worst outcome of which is superior to the worst outcome of the others (pp. 152-3). Rawls says there are three chief features of situations that give plausibility to the use of this extremely conservative decision rule (p. 154). Without detailing those reasons here, I will say that a rule such as this makes sense when the risks are extremely high and the possibility of assessing the probability of the occurrence of these risks does not exist. For those in the original position that is the problem—the principles of justice they will choose have a bearing on whether, for example, they as individuals may end up as slaves, or impoverished and destitute. And the opportunity for assessing the probability of these consequences occurring under any of the alternative principles of justice under consideration does not exist since the people in the original position are working under a veil of ignorance.

Hence, using the maximin rule for guidance, the people in the original position, Rawls says, will assess the possible worst consequences that might occur under each of the alternative principles of justice being considered. Which consequences are deemed worst is, of course, partially a function of the values of the people in the original position, and whose values are a function of the Aristotelian Principle.

For the people in the original position, one set of principles (listed below) has worst outcomes that are superior to the worst outcomes under the other principles Rawls considers. The other principles, which are largely various forms of utilitarianism, tend to expose people to the following sorts of risks: (1) The operation of the economic system under some principles might be such that a person ends up destitute, without even his basic needs taken care of (p. 156). (2) Personal and civil rights might be constrained so that greater economic gains might be achieved even though the society might have achieved an overall satisfactory level of economic output (pp. 156, 542). (3) Some unacceptable principles would permit restrictions on equality of opportunity for the sake of economic gains. This tradeoff is unacceptable since the price is barring people from gaining offices and jobs in which they could experience "the realization of self which comes from a skillful and devoted exercise of social duties. They would be deprived of one of the main forms of human good" (p. 84). (4) And the unacceptable principles might allow such extremely unequal social conditions that the relative inequalities would undermine self-respect (pp. 178-179, 534). The people in the original position, however, because of the value they place on self-respect, prefer to avoid at almost any cost social conditions that undermine self-respect (p. 440). (For a general discussion in the book see sections 26-30.)

The principles that emerge from the decision process thus win by a process of elimination. The principles of justice are:

First Principle
Each person is to have an equal right to the most extensive total system of equal basic liberties compatible with a similar system of liberty for all. [*Liberty Principle*]

Second Principle
Social and economic inequalities are to be arranged so that they are both:

a.   to the greatest benefit of the least advantaged, consistent with the just savings principle [*Difference Principle*], and
b.   attached to offices and positions open to all under conditions of fair equality of opportunity. [*Fair Equality of Opportunity Principle*]

First Priority Rule (The Priority of Liberty)
The principles of justice are to be ranked in lexical order, and therefore liberty can be restricted only for the sake of liberty. There are two cases:

    a.   a less extensive liberty must strengthen the total system of liberty shared by all;

    b.   a less than equal liberty must be acceptable to those with the lesser liberty.

Second Priority Rule (The Priority of Justice over Efficiency and Welfare)
The second principle of justice is lexically prior to the principle of efficiency and to that of maximizing the sum of advantages; and fair opportunity is prior to the difference principle. There are two cases:

    a.   an inequality of opportunity must enhance the opportunities of those with the lesser opportunity;

    b.   an excessive rate of saving must on balance mitigate the burden of those bearing this hardship (pp. 302-303).

Beyond these principles Rawls says those in the original position would establish another general principle that different generations have duties and obligations to one another just as contemporaries do (p. 293). This principle would be adopted because of the following considerations. Since the parties in the original position had no information as to which generation they may belong they had to choose principles the "consequences of which they are prepared to live with whatever generation they turn out to belong to" (p. 137). Rawls also adds a "motivational assumption" as part of the description of the parties in the original position:

The parties are thought of as representing continuing lines of claims, as being so to speak deputies for a kind of everlasting moral agent or institution. They need not take into account its entire life span in perpetuity, but their goodwill stretches over at least two generations ... [W]e may think of the parties as heads of families, and therefore as having a desire to further the welfare of their nearest descendents (p. 128).

It logically follows that the above duty would be adopted in the original position.

    Two principles specify in greater detail the nature of the duty owed by one generation to another. First is the savings principle, which holds:

Each generation must not only preserve the gains of culture and civilization, and maintain intact those just institutions that have been established, but it must also put aside in each period of time a suitable amount of real capital accumulation. This savings may take various forms from net investment in machinery and other means of production to investment in learning and education (p. 285).

Rawls says the principle "can be regarded as an understanding between generations to carry their fair share of the burden of realizing and preserving a just society" (p. 289).

The second principle is the principle of paternalism: "We must choose for others as we have reason to believe they would choose for themselves if they were at the age of reason and deciding rationally" (p. 209). Finally, note should be made that Rawls sees those in the original position as adopting as a general principle a duty not to harm or injure others (p. 114).

The Principles and Education

The basic liberties referred to in the liberty principle include the right to vote and be eligible for public office, freedom of speech and assembly, liberty of conscience and freedom of thought; freedom of the person along with the right to hold personal property; and freedom from arbitrary arrest and seizure as defined by the concept of the rule of law (p. 61). This first principle is lexically prior to the other principles, which means that liberty can only be restricted for the sake of liberty itself (a point Rawls does not elaborate on with any great clarity), not in order to advance, for example, economic well-being (p. 244). This principle constrains the other principles and must be satisfied before implementation of the other principles is carried out.

The liberty principle only requires that there be "formal" equality of liberty, and Rawls admits that the "worth of the liberties" may be unequal due to such circumstances as unequal wealth. In other words, while all may formally have a right to equal liberty, differences in wealth permitted by the difference principle (discussed below) may make it impossible for everybody equally to make use of that right (p. 204).

Rawls is troubled by this problem of the unequal worth of liberties and adds, without providing a supporting argument, that society should make sure that "those similarly endowed and motivated should have roughly the same chance of attaining positions of political authority irrespective of their economic and social class" (p. 225).

As suggestions for how this might be done, Rawls says that in his ideal society government could make sure that wealth is not so unequally distributed as to destroy the fair value of the liberties; it could assure people of the means to be informed about political issues; and it could subsidize political debate and the political parties to avoid allowing the political process becoming the captive of wealthy contributors (pp. 225-226).

No mention is made of education as a means of assuring the fair value of political liberties despite the fact that Rawls had earlier recognized that "the inability to take advantage of one's rights and opportunities as a result of poverty and *ignorance*" (emphasis added) affects the worth of liberty (p. 204). It would seem that education would be a most natural way to assure that background environmental factors do not place an unfair burden on people of equal ability and motivation who seek political stakes.

Because of these considerations, it is reasonable to conclude that Rawls may not have deliberately omitted any reference to education as a means of assuring the equal worth of liberties. I would like to suggest that education might very well have been included as one of the ways of securing fair equality of liberty. Indeed, intuitively, education seems to be such an important means of securing fair equality of liberty—it is hard to imagine the worth of liberty being equal if some are educated and some are not—that the liberty principle must be read to imply a right to an education.

The opportunity principle, the second part of the second principle, provides that "social and economic inequalities are to be arranged so that they are both attached to offices and positions open to all under conditions of fair equality of opportunity" (p. 302). Rawls provides this gloss on the principle:

The thought here is that positions are to be not only open in a formal sense, but that all should have a fair chance to attain them. Offhand it is not clear what is meant, but we might say that those with similar abilities and skills have similar life chances. More specifically, assuming that there is a distribution of natural assets, those who are at the same level of talent and ability, and have the same willingness to use them, should have the same prospects of success regardless of their initial place in the social system, that is, irrespective of the income class into which they are born. In all sectors of society there should be roughly equal prospects of culture and achievement for everyone similarly motivated and endowed. The expectations for those with the same abilities and aspirations should not be affected by their social class (p. 73).

Rawls then adds: "Furthermore, the principle of fair equality of opportunity can be only imperfectly carried out, at least as long as the institution of the family exists" (p. 74). Later Rawls asks:

Is the family to be abolished then? Taken by itself and given certain primacy, the idea of equal opportunity inclines in this direction. But within the context of the theory of justice as a whole, there is much less urgency to take this course. The acknowledgement of the difference principle redefines the grounds for social inequalities as conceived in the system of liberal equality; and when the principles of fraternity and redress are allowed their appropriate weight, the natural distribution of assets and the contingencies of social circumstances can more easily be accepted (pp. 511-512; also p. 301).

Thus instead of seeking to abolish the family, Rawls proposes several not completely effective ways of bringing about fair equality of opportunity, including the following: "Chances to acquire cultural knowledge and skills should not depend upon one's class position, and so the school system, whether public or private, should be designed to even out class barriers" (p. 73). And again:

I also assume that there is fair (as opposed to formal) equality of opportunity. This means that in addition to maintaining the usual kinds of social overhead capital, the government tries to insure equal chances of education and culture for persons similarly endowed and motivated either by subsidizing private schools or by establishing a public school system (p. 275).

These passages imply a right to an education. This conclusion is underscored by the fact that one of the very reasons for adopting the opportunity principle in the first place is to assure that the Aristotelian Principle is given a chance to flourish (p. 84). It only seems natural then that educational services be provided to implement the opportunity principle.

This implied right to an education, it might be noted, is a right that must be satisfied and may not be frustrated by income shortages. Professor Frank I. Michelman makes the point elegantly:

But by attaching this right to the lexically preferred opportunity principle, Rawls must mean that it has to be satisfied before the difference principle can be allowed to operate—that compensatory satisfaction of the opportunity interest is prerequisite to allowing any income inequalities to arise in the market place. It seems to follow that no one may be precluded from the requisite education by income shortage; and this would be, then an insurance right.[9]

Before turning to the difference principle, we should take note of the implications of several of the more minor principles. As for the savings principle, the many technical problems involved in using this principle will be put aside in favor of focusing on the simple point that the principle obliges one generation to pass on to the next real capital which is defined not just in terms of factories and machines but also as "the knowledge and culture, as well as the techniques and skills, that make possible just institutions and the fair value of liberty" (p. 288). Once again a Rawls principle establishes a right on the part of children to the maintenance of educational institutions and the provision of educational services. In this case, however, the right is not the right of an individual but a right held by an entire generation. That is, the savings principle establishes no claim for an education on the part of any single individual as it only requires the intellectual capital held in trust by one generation be passed on to some people in the next generation. Although the principle creates no entitlement in any single individual, it does tend to reinforce the duties owed to specific individuals created by the other principles.

The second more specific principle to emerge from the original position which deals with justice between generations (among other matters) is the principle of paternalism: "We must choose for others as we have reason to believe they would choose for themselves if they were at the age of reason and deciding rationally" (p. 209). Rawls adds:

Paternalistic decisions are to be guided by the individual's own settled preferences and interests insofar as they are not irrational, or failing a knowledge of these, by the theory of primary goods. As we know less and less about a person, we act for him as we would act for ourselves from the standpoint of the original position. We try to get for him the things he presumably wants whatever else he wants. We must be able to argue that within the development or the recovery of his rational powers the individual in question will accept our decision on his behalf and agree with us that we did the best thing for him (p. 249).

This principle suggests that both government and a child's parent have a duty to provide the child with an education: Any child who grew up without an education which could have led to the formation and realization of life plans by the child in keeping with the Aristotelian Principle would have a strong basis on which to complain. Providing a child with an education would seem to be required if we are to get the consent of the child, upon reaching maturity, that we did the best thing for him. Once again an adult duty implies a corresponding right to an education.

All this is underscored by yet another principle, the principle requiring us not to harm or injure another (p. 114). Rawls provides no explication of this principle other than calling it one of the "natural duties," but we might say with Joel Feinberg that the notion of harm can include the idea of failing to provide something to somebody which they need.[10] If this is so, then once again a basis has been found for implying a right to an education—failure to provide will clearly stunt the realization of the Aristotelian Principle. However, we must be wary of following this line since Rawls calls the duty not to do harm a "negative duty," which suggests it should not be read so as to impose on the parents (or state) the positive duty of providing an education (p. 114). Nevertheless, the idea that neglecting children does them harm is so much a part of our thinking that it would be surprising if Rawls objected in this instance to the Feinberg notion of harm. Besides, the principle of mutual aid suggests that we have a positive duty to protect people, including children, from great harm, provided that the sacrifice and hazards to the person owing the duty are not very great (pp. 438-439, 114). Educating children so that they are protected from the risk of not being able to realize life plans consistent with the Aristotelian Principle would seem a duty that can be fulfilled without the sort of sacrifice and hazard that would excuse one from doing his duty (pp. 338-339).

To this point Rawls's moral principles appear not to be strikingly different from those currently accepted. Most importantly, Rawls accepts the concept of equal opportunity as backed up by the provision of educational services. However, Rawls would mitigate the results of a system of equal opportunity by the application of his "difference principle," which holds that the social and economic inequalities resulting from the implementation of the liberty and equal opportunity principles must be arranged so that they are to the greatest advantage of the least advantaged. That is, the distribution of primary goods resulting from the operation of the political-economic-social system must be such that the least well-off have obtained the maximum amount possible under the existing conditions of the society.

Rawls suggests that the least advantaged might be defined in several different ways, e.g., the least advantaged are those unskilled workers with average or lower incomes than that of all unskilled workers (p. 98). While there are other ways of defining the worst off group, an important point is that Rawls is concerned with "representative persons" in that worst-off group, however defined. He is not talking about, it seems at first glance, the atypical person in the worst-off group (p. 64).

With this in mind Rawls can be read as saying, in simple terms, that inequalities in the distribution of primary goods are justified only if the representative persons in the worst-off group prefer their life expectations under an unequal distribution of goods than to their expectations if goods were equally distributed. The unequal distribution of goods might mean that those who are getting more will have been given an incentive to be more inventive, productive, and effective with the result that the worst-off group reaps the benefits of the increased productivity of the economy. Instead of everybody having $10, now some people have $20 (the better off) but the worst-off now have $15 (pp. 75-83). As for the difference principle and the provision of education, Rawls says educational resources would be allocated with a view to improving the long-term expectations of the least favored. Such an approach would not assure that all individuals would be given even a basic education. As Rawls says, "if this end is attained by giving more attention to the better endowed, it is permissible; otherwise not" (pp. 101, 311). The basic idea is to make the greater abilities of the better endowed a social asset to work for the common advantage (pp. 101, 107).

There are many complications and difficulties involved in working with the difference principle including defining the worst-off group; deciding when taxation of the rich to increase the minimum of the worst-off results in disincentive effects to the detriment of the poor; and deciding if the best-off might still be taxed more to the advantage of the worst-off. Beyond these difficulties in the application of the principle, the principle apparently permits some unusual consequences to take place. For one, it may permit and even require a billion-dollar advantage to be given to the best-off as an incentive for a slight increase in production which results in a miniscule advantage for the worst-off. Hence, great inequalities in wealth may be possible under the principle. Rawls admits of this possibility but argues that the full operation of the principle of fair equality of opportunity should preclude such an occurrence (p. 158). Next the difference principle might require that enormous efforts be made to maximize the level of income of the worst-off even if that results in an overall drop in the aggregate wealth of the society. If the worst-off are better off in a poorer society than in an overall richer society, then this is what the difference principle requires. Third, the level of income available to the worst-off in a society is contingent on the wealth of that society. No fixed amount is assured the worst-off. Fourth, the principle only deals in terms of maximizing the "average" income for a representative person from the worst-off group; hence some in that group by definition must have less than the average for the group. Fifth, the principle does not assure that people in the worst-off group will have their basic needs met if and when they arise. This is so in part because: (1) Some people in the worst-off group will have only incomes below the average for the group; and (2) even the average income for the group may not be satisfactory to meet all basic needs, e.g., both health care and educational services.

The last point must have troubled Rawls, for in several passages in which he discusses the policy implications of his principles, he suggests that legislatures may be required by the difference principle to take care of basic needs such as health by providing special grants for health care (p. 275). Rawls never explains why his difference principle might require the meeting of these basic needs, but attempts have been made to reconstruct Rawls's philosophy so that these basic needs must be taken care of before the liberty, fair equality, and difference principles are allowed their normal operation. The gist of the argument is that if individuals in the original position should rationally exhibit such a pronounced conservatism to lead them to the maximin principle in choosing principles of justice, it would be logical to expect of them to adopt a principle assuring that basic needs will be met if and when they arise so that basic rights, liberties, and opportunities may be effectively enjoyed and self-respect maintained.[11] Thus children under this conception must be provided with an education as this might be conceived as a basic need. And this would be crucial for our purposes if Rawls had not already provided a sound basis for assuring children of an education pursuant to the liberty and equal-opportunity principles as well as the savings principle and the principle of paternalism.

Implications

While Rawls has built into his philosophy a general position on education, we need to probe more deeply to uncover the full implications. As will be seen, Rawls's philosophy lays the ground for recognition of a special conception of the right to an education which in turn has important implications for such important matters as financing education. Additionally, Rawls's philosophy speaks to such issues as the purposes and methods of education.

Right to an Education

There are two main dimensions to any possible definition of a right to an education which are captured by asking the questions (1) Against whom does the right run?; and (2) What does it ask of the person (institution) which owes the duty to the one who enjoys the right? There are three possible answers to the first question—the government or the parents of the child, or perhaps both.

Very roughly, there are at least four possible answers to the second question. Either the child is owed certain inputs—money, facilities, services to be provided at some minimum level regardless of the likely effect on achievement; or the child is owed a provision of that input which according to present knowledge is reasonably calculated to result in a certain level of achievement; or the duty is to assure each child of a certain minimum level of achievement; or the duty might be to assure the child that his family and social background will not be a major determinant of the level of his achievement.

From what has already been said about Rawls's principles, it can be seen that Rawls strongly implies the existence of a right on the part of each child which runs against the government, and the duty of the government is to assure that the family and social background of the child will not be a major determinant of the level of his achievement. [It might be noted here that Rawls assumes that government can meet its educational obligations by either providing a public school system or by subsidizing private education (p. 275).] With regard to the operation of the liberty principle, Rawls has said that to assure equal worth of liberties, those similarly endowed and motivated should have roughly the same chance of attaining positions of political authority irrespective of their economic and social class (p. 225). He has also made similar comment with regard to the opportunity principle (pp. 73, 275). What Rawls excludes is that the achievement of those who suffer from handicaps of genetic or traumatic origin be equal with those of children who are normal (pp. 73, 101). And, that it is the government which owes the duty created by the liberty and opportunity principles is obvious since these principles were created to apply to the basic institutions of the society. When we turn to the principle of paternalism and the principle of not doing harm, however, we can see that parents also have a duty to educate their children. However, with regard to these principles it might be argued the duty owed is only to provide students with certain input since it hardly seems plausible to ask parents to make sure their social and economic background not be a conditioning factor in the achievement of their children.

Turning back to the governmental duty, Rawls's right to an education leads to the conclusion that government will have to provide certain children with compensatory education to overcome their social and economic backgrounds in order that only their natural ability and motivation will be factors in determining their life chances. Thus our present systems of educational finance, which make unlikely this kind of compensatory education, our present systems of tracking and ability grouping, our present practice of providing non-English-speaking students with an all-English school program, and our present practice of pushing many students out of school once they are beyond compulsory attendance age would all be deemed morally impermissible. And most obviously discrimination on the basis of race or sex would be precluded. As for education of the mentally retarded, Rawls seems only to require that the social-class background of the mentally retarded not be a determinant in their life chances, but he does not require educational programs that will aid the mentally retarded to become as competent as normal children—even if we had the educational technology to accomplish such a feat. Finally, access to higher education could not be conditioned by the student's social and economic background, but we shall see momentarily that other considerations arising out of Rawls's principles affect who will be given access to this expensive form of education.

The Right to an Education and Rational Life Planning

Since the ultimate good of an individual is the successful execution of a rational life plan which fulfills the Aristotelian Principle, the notion of a right to an education, the principle of paternalism, and the duty not to harm lend support to the conclusion that a duty exists to help children achieve this good. The harm that might result would involve damage to the child's sense of self-worth—the most important primary good—since without having developed a capacity for rational planning as well as a rational plan, the child would leave home to enter a society arranged and designed for people who had both that capacity and a plan. Anybody who did not have these characteristics would be a fish out of water inevitably leading to a sense of inadequacy.

The duty to aid students in rational life planning would lead schools to assist those students in choosing that plan that best fulfills the Aristotelian Principle and that is consistent with the principles of justice. Now some of the work of choosing a life (and then of course helping a student obtain the necessary education to realize his life plan) is made simpler by the fact that the society is more supportive of some life plans than others (pp. 31, 259, 425, 449).

Even with the shaping influence of the environment on life planning, there is still considerable room for choice, and here the most difficult part of the school's responsibility arises. Although Rawls assumes that people will not establish a single, dominant end for their life plans, because of the operation of the Aristotelian Principle, no one person can pursue every end which the workings of the Aristotelian Principle might motivate him to seek. There is neither time, opportunity, nor money available for life plans that involve the development of each of a person's potentialities (p. 523). [Nor can an individual plan upon an unlimited development of selected potentialities as there are ever increased costs in pursuing this route (p. 428).] Choices have to be made, and paternalism suggests that advice is to be given. But what sort of advice should be given is made complicated by the fact that what is good for the child is not always easily discernible and by the fact that what the child may want may be inconsistent with the demands of the difference principle. For example, assume a child wants to become an engineer but lacks the requisite mathematical ability to become a good engineer; the difference principle would counsel that it would be to the advantage of the worst-off in society to spend the money on training only those who are better endowed, rather than those who simply have a desire and modest ability to be an engineer (p. 101). What the child wants and the advice we give will conflict, and we are left with a conflict of rights: the right of the individual and that of society (p. 448). Since Rawls says that life plans must be developed within the constraints of the principles of justice, presumably he would conclude that the school neither advise nor help the child to become an engineer.

The school could not, however, force a child into a particular occupation. The principles of liberty and of opportunity both point in the direction of a notion of liberty to choose our occupation (pp. 272, 274). It would be inconsistent with the priority of these two principles over the difference principle to justify forcing students into particular occupations in the name of the difference principle. Hence, the school might have an effective veto over an occupational choice, but it may not actually choose an occupation for the student. But this veto itself might appear to be inconsistent with the priority of liberty over the difference principle, yet we are forced to conclude that this more limited way of violating the priority rankings is necessary: Not to permit this sort of veto would result in vast sums of money being spent on educational programs at the demand of students and at the expense of the worst off in society. As has been concluded elsewhere with regard to the tension between liberty and the difference principle:

[T]he priority rules, and the idea of lexical orderings, are not to be understood in crudely fundamentalist or vindictively literal way, but rather to be taken more loosely as a way of lending a shape and structure to the entire doctrine, which is to remain supple and not hidebound.[12]

Once the child has chosen a life plan consistent with the difference principle, however, the schools incur an obligation to aid in the realization of the plan. As discussed above, the principle of paternalism, and perhaps the notion of a right to an education, impose on schools the duty to help train a student in those abilities and skills needed to carry out the life plan. Stated differently, the duty is to aid the student to become a "good" person in the sense that the student will have, to a higher degree than the average, characteristics or properties which it is rational for citizens to want of a person who has entered on a specific role such as that of doctor or farmer (p. 435).

The Moral Content of the School Program

Beyond training a student to realize his life plans, Rawls's principles have important implications for the moral content of the educational program. While the usual question we ask today is whether the public schools should be permitted to attempt to provide a moral education, the question to ask of Rawls is whether schools, public or private, are morally required to provide moral education? Or more specifically, must schools in Rawls's ideal society attempt to bring about on the part of their students a commitment to the principles of justice which form the basic charter of the society?

Before starting to provide a direct answer to the question, it should be noted that Rawls assumes that a commitment to the principles of justice would naturally develop, to an extent, in his ideal society. Rawls believes the environment the child would live in would trigger the operation of three psychological laws of moral development that would lead to an early arousal of the desire to conform to moral standards even before the child achieves an adequate understanding of the reasons for these norms (pp. 458, 462-478, 490-496).[13]

But despite the operation of these natural psychological laws, Rawls says that whether or not the citizens of the ideal society are committed to the principles of justice should not be left to chance. The problem of stability of the society is so important that certain institutions should be established which are to foster the virtue of justice and to discourage desires and aspirations incompatible with it (pp. 32, 261). Among the institutions that would serve this function are the schools (pp. 278, 515). The schools would supplement the automatic psychological processes mentioned above by using such techniques as reinforcement, classical conditioning, highly abstract reasoning, and the use of human exemplars (p. 461). In sum, because a sense of justice is a collective good and because the natural learning processes are not sufficient to bring about this sense of justice, formal schooling should be used to aid in fostering this disposition.

The conclusion that teaching to encourage a sense of justice should be done can be also based on another line of reasoning: not only is it a collective good for children to come to have a sense of justice and other moral virtues, it is also congruent with the children's own good; and, if this is so, the principle of paternalism, if not the notion of a right to an education, leads to the conclusion that teaching to cultivate a sense of justice be done.

This argument hinges on establishing that having a sense of justice is in the interest of the child—is consistent with the child's own good. Rawls offers several arguments in support of this point. Acting from the principles of justice expresses our nature as free and moral persons: It is a form of moral self-actualization. Participating in the well-ordered society is itself a form of self-realization, but to fully participate, one must be committed to the principles of justice. And not to act on the principles of justice can lead to injuries to our friends and associates, people we do not wish to harm (pp. 570-572).

Assuming schools do have an obligation to foster a sense of justice, what does this purpose entail? Rawls defines a sense of justice as follows:

First, it leads us to accept the just institutions that apply to us and from which we and our associates have benefited. We want to do our part in maintaining these arrangements. We tend to feel guilty when we do not honor our duties and obligations, . . . Secondly, sense of justice gives rise to a willingness to work for (or at least not to oppose) the setting up of just institutions, and for the reform of existing ones when justice requires it. We desire to act on the natural duty to advance just arrangements (p. 474).

The natural duty of justice requires us "to support and to further the arrangements that satisfy these principles. . . ." (p. 335). Thus instruction would be designed to cultivate a sense of justice as just defined. But Rawls provides only a little guidance as to how the sense of justice might formally be fostered.

To this point my interpretation of Rawls leaves him open to the charges that his philosophy leads to the development of an educational system that encourages the development of moral dispositions without regard to whether the student freely comes to an acceptance of these virtues and that students are to be trained to mindlessly acquiesce in the existing society, well-ordered and just though it may be.

But the impression of mindless conformity to an overbearing state which is induced by an education designed to get children to internalize Rawls's various principles and duties is not a fair reading of Rawls. First, the duty to support just institutions itself logically leads to a duty to oppose unjust institutions—a duty Rawls recognizes in several places (pp. 363, 381, 519). Rawls expects his citizens in the ideal state to oppose unjust laws by civil disobedience, if necessary, and thus he also expects those citizens to reach their own independent judgments as to the fairness of their own laws and institutions (pp. 195-196, 317-377).

Finally, we should note this passage:

The moral education is education for autonomy. In due course everyone will know why he would adopt the principles of justice and how they are derived from the conditions that characterize his being an equal in a society of moral persons. It follows that in accepting these principles on this basis we are not influenced primarily by tradition and authority, or the opinion of others. However necessary these agencies may be in order for us to reach complete understanding, we eventually come to hold a conception of right on reasonable grounds that we can set out independently for ourselves (p. 516, also pp. 496, 520).

We are thus compelled to the conclusion that a central purpose of education must be the cultivation of a capacity for moral reasoning. Cultivating this capacity is not only important as part of the effort to build into the society an intelligent capacity to keep the society in conformity with the principles of justice, but it is also an important part of the child's own self-development as defined by the Aristotelian Principle (p. 445).

Methods of Education

In several places Rawls asserts that the methods of education must be regulated by the principles of justice (pp. 250, 514-515). In turn, the principles lead Rawls to offer both positive and negative prescriptions.

First, the negative prescription. The negative prescription arises out of Rawls's discussion of the principle of paternalism in which he says that in acting on the basis of paternalism, "We must be able to argue that with the development or the recovery of his rational powers the individual in question will accept our decision on his behalf and agree with us that we did the best thing for him" (p. 249). But Rawls adds that the principle of paternalism must not be interpreted as a license to assault a child's mind and character even if such an assault offers the prospect of securing consent to the principles instilled by such methods (pp. 249-250). Thus Rawls rules out techniques of indoctrination and brainwashing as methods of education. Presumably he adds this limitation to the principle of paternalism because of yet another duty—the duty of mutual respect.

The duty of mutural respect requires, among other things, that we be "prepared to give reasons for our actions whenever the interests of others are materially affected" (p. 337). Thus, in carrying out an educational program on behalf of a child, we are required to give reasons which we consider to be sound and which will enable the child to accept the program we are offering (pp. 337-338). This stricture Rawls qualifies when he writes:

Thus no one's moral convictions are the result of coercive indoctrination. Instruction is throughout reasoned *as the development of understanding permits*, just as the natural duty of mutual respect requires. None of the ideals, principles, and precepts upheld in the society take unfair advantage of human weakness. A person's sense of justice is not a compulsive psychological mechanism cleverly installed by those in authority in order to insure his unswerving compliance with rules designed to advance their interests (p. 515). (Emphasis added.)

It will be recalled that Rawls says, "moral education is education for autonomy" (p. 516).

While Rawls stresses the importance of reason, he also acknowledges that "reinforcement," or "instrumental conditioning" and "classical conditioning," may be necessary techniques of moral instruction. Prior to the age of reason these techniques may be the most efficient in starting the process of learning. Further, reinforcement and conditioning would not be tantamount to "coercive indoctrination" and would have been carried out in conformity with the principles of justice. Besides, reason ultimately will be introduced into the educational process and "in due course everyone will know why he would adopt the principles of justice and how they are derived from the conditions that characterize his being an equal in a society of moral persons" (p. 516).

Finally, a few words on authority in education are warranted. Because of Rawls's acceptance of the principle of paternalism, he clearly presupposes that adults—whether the state or parents—have authority to control a child's education. This authority is based on the assumption that the reasoning and moral capacities of children are immature as well as the fact that children lack sufficient knowledge to care for themselves. But these very factors not only create the authority but also the duty to exercise the authority. If adults were to let children control their own education and things turned out badly for the child, the adult might be faulted for failure to protect the child from harm. In sum, the principle of paternalism imposes on adults not only authority but a duty to control the child's education.

However, Rawls also subscribes to the duty of mutual respect, the assumption that children are moral persons and that planning and determining one's life plan is one of the more important liberties a person enjoys. Further, even the principle of paternalism requires that the adult give due consideration to the settled, rational preferences of the child. All this points in the direction of granting considerable influence and weight to the child's own preferences with regard to his education.

Thus the vectors of Rawls's principles seem to point in different directions: one line of reasoning toward total adult control of the child's education, the other toward significant control by the child over his own education. Reconciliation probably should take the following form: The older the child becomes, the more mature and developed his capacity for rational planning and moral judgment, the more control of his education is to be placed in his own hands. This is hardly a remarkable conclusion nor one inconsistent with the existing considered judgments. Nevertheless, it is an important conclusion that in the day-to-day operation of schools, we tend to lose sight of and abuse. Rawls reminds us of the conclusion and the reasons that support it.

Conclusions

This essay has attempted to establish the plausibility of interpreting *A Theory of Justice* as supporting the notion of a right to an education. The notion of a right to an education may be disturbing enough to some people, but in addition Rawls seems to support a moral obligation on the part of schools not only to help students develop their own rational life plans but also morally to educate those students. Rawls can be read on this last point as supporting such an idea not only because it is good for the society but also because it is in the interest of the child living in the ideal society. Rawls does, however, oppose using brainwashing and indoctrination to bring about a blind and unthinking acceptance of the principles of justice. As much as possible, reason should be used in the process of formal schooling, and the end result should be children who not only accept the principles of justice but also have a capacity for moral reasoning.

Thus Rawls's philosophy of education points towards the development of a Rawlsian ideal person. This individual would be a morally and nonmorally self-actualized person. This individual would have all those moral virtues other members of the society would wish him to have as well as a set of developed skills and abilities others would want in that person given his social role (pp. 435-436, 443). It is the task of formal education to work toward this kind of ideal person.

It is important to note, however, that Rawls's philosophy is not a theory of perfectionism. Perfectionist theories direct us "to arrange institutions and to define the duties and obligations of individuals so as to maximize the achievement of human excellence in art, science, and culture" (p. 325). Perfectionist theories are teleological in that they begin with an a priori end such as some ideal of the person and then develop principles to maximize realization of that end. Rawls's theory does not begin with an a priori notion of an ideal human; its starting point is the narrower assumption about what is good for people, and from that assumption the principles of justice are derived. Only when the principles of justice are in place is Rawls prepared to define an ideal of the person (p. 261). This is a distinction of great importance for the liberty of the person. Perfectionist theories could easily lead to severe constraints on children's liberty as education is imposed to achieve an ideal of the person (pp. 327-328), whereas Rawls's philosophy insists first of all on the protection of children's liberties and requires that education take place within this constraint. To the extent children under Rawls's philosophy are pushed toward a conception of an ideal moral person—an ideal they might not at first freely have chosen to pursue—it is done as a way of furthering commitment to principles assumed to be just. Ultimately, of course, Rawls assumes the child will himself freely accept his commitment to the principles.

Notes

1. John Rawls, *A Theory of Justice* (Cambridge, Mass.: Harvard University Press, 1971). All page references in the text of the essay are to *A Theory of Justice.* Portions reprinted with permission from the Harvard University Press. © 1971 by the President and Fellows of Harvard College and Oxford University Press.

2. *San Antonio Independent School District v. Rodriguez*, 411 U.S. 1 (1973).

3. Stanley Herr, "Retarded Children and the Law," *Syracuse Law Review* 23 (1972): 995; Children's Defense Fund of the Washington Research Project, 14C., *Children Out of School in America* (Cambridge, Mass.: Children's Defense Fund, 1974).

4. *Hobson v. Hansen*, 269 F. Supp. 401 (D.DC 1967) *aff'd sub nom, Smuck v. Hobson*, 408 F.2d 175 (CD Cir 1969) (*en banc*).

5. Tyll van Geel, "The Right to Be Taught Standard English: Exploring the Implications of *Lau v. Nichols* for Black Americans," *Syracuse Law Review* 25 (1974): 863.

6. James S. Coleman et al., *Equality of Educational Opportunity* (Washington, D.C.: U.S. Department of Health, Education, and Welfare, U.S. Government Printing Office, 1966); F. Mosteller and D. Moynihan, eds., *On Equality of Educational Opportunity* (New York: Random House, 1972).

7. Daniel Bell, "On Meritocracy and Equality," *The Public Interest* 29 (Fall 1972): 28, 42.

8. Christober Jencks et al., *Inequality: A Reassessment of the Effect of Family and Schooling in America* (New York: Basic Books, 1972).

9. Frank I. Michelman, "In Pursuit of Constitutional Welfare Rights: One View of Rawls' Theory of Justice," *University of Pennsylvania Law Review* 121 (1973): 962, 966. © Copyright *University of Pennsylvania Law Review.*

10. Joel Feinberg, *Social Philosophy* (Englewood Cliffs, N.J.: Prentice-Hall, 1973), p. 30.

11. Michelman, "In Pursuit of Constitutional Welfare Rights," p. 991.

12. Ibid., p. 973, note beginning on p. 972.

13. In developing his theory of moral development, Rawls has borrowed from several sources. He cites William McDougall, *An Introduction to Social Psychology* (London: Methuen, 1908); Jean Piaget, *The Moral Judgment of the Child*, trans. Marjorie Gabian (London: Kagen Paul, Trench, Trubner, 1932); and Lawrence Kohlberg, "The Development of Children's Orientation toward a Moral Order: 1. Sequence in the Development of Moral Thought," *Vita Humana* 6 (1963); and "Stage and Sequence: The Cognitive Developmental Approach to Socialization," in *Handbook of Socialization Theory and Research*, ed. D.A. Goslin (Chicago: Rand McNally, 1969), chap. 6.

About the Contributors

Joel S. Berke is Director of the Education Policy Research Institute of the Educational Testing Service. Among his relevant publications is *Answers to Inequity: An Analysis of the New School Finance* (1974). He will spend the next academic year as a Guggenheim Fellow writing about the interactions between policy change and the governance of American public education.

Michael O. Boss, deceased. Formerly of the University of Oregon.

Fred G. Burke is Commissioner of Education, State of New Jersey. He was formerly Commissioner of Education in Rhode Island. He has been on the faculty of Ohio Wesleyan University, Syracuse University, and the State University of New York at Buffalo. Among his publications are *Africa's Quest for Order, Local Government and Politics in Uganda, Transformation of East Africa*, and *Pre-Planning in Tanganyika*.

Samuel Halperin is Director of the Institute for Educational Leadership at George Washington University, Washington, D.C. He was formerly Deputy Assistant Secretary for Legislation of HEW (1966-69) and Assistant U.S. Commissioner of Education for Legislation (1964-66).

Willis D. Hawley is Associate Director of the Institute of Policy Sciences and Public Affairs and Associate Professor of Policy Sciences and Political Science at Duke University. His current research deals with change in public organizations and the impact of schooling on political learning. His books include *Theoretical Perspectives on Urban Politics, Improving the Quality of Urban Management, Nonpartisan Elections and the Case for Party Politics*, and *The Search for Community Power*.

Paul T. Hill is the Director of the National Institute of Education's Compensatory Education Study. A political scientist, he is a former APSA Congressional Fellow, and worked in the Policy Research Division of OEO and on the HUD National Housing Subsidy Policy Study.

Donna E. Shalala is Associate Professor and Chairwoman of the Program in Politics and Education, Teachers College, Columbia University. She currently is serving on the Municipal Assistance Corporation for the City of New York. She received her Ph.D. from the Maxwell Graduate School, Syracuse University. A John Simon Guggenheim Fellow in 1975-76, she has written extensively on the political economy of schools and state and local government.

Harvey Tucker is a Research Associate of the Center for Educational Policy and Management, and Assistant Professor of Political Science, University of Oregon. He currently is studying patterns of governance in public school districts.

Tyll van Geel is Assistant Professor in the College of Education, University of Rochester. His primary scholarly concern is in the area of law and educational policy, on which he has written several articles. D.C. Heath will be publishing his book entitled *Authority to Control the School Program*, and he is a recipient of a Spencer Fellowship awarded by the National Academy of Education.

Mary Frase Williams is an Assistant Professor, Program in Politics and Education, Teachers College, Columbia University.

L.A. Wilson II is an Assistant Professor of Political Science at the University of Nevada, Las Vegas, Nevada. He is currently engaged in research on public policy in the areas of education and crime.

Thomas R. Wolanin is Assistant Professor of Political Science at the University of Wisconsin-Madison. He is currently on leave serving on the staff of the House Education and Labor Committee. He received his doctorate from Harvard University and is the author of *Presidential Advisory Commissions: Truman to Nixon* (1975) and co-author of *Congress and the Colleges: The National Politics of Higher Education* (1976).

L. Harmon Zeigler is Professor of Political Science and Program Director, Center for Educational Policy and Management, University of Oregon. He is senior author of the volume *Governing American Schools*.

About the Editors

Samuel K. Gove is Director of the Institute of Government and Public Affairs and Professor of Political Science, University of Illinois. He is the advisor for the Public Administration Program. His academic interests are state and local government and politics, especially in the field of higher education. He is co-author of "Research on Higher Education Administration and Policy: An Uneven Report," published in the *Public Administration Review* (1975), and "The Politics of Public Higher Education: Illinois," published in *AAUP Bulletin* (1974). He serves as education co-editor for *Policy Studies Journal.*

Frederick M. Wirt is Professor of Political Science, University of Illinois, since Fall, 1975. Previously taught at Denison University, University of California at Berkeley and University of Maryland Baltimore County. His academic interests include urban politics and the politics of education. He was Research Political Scientist, Institute of Governmental Studies, University of California, Berkeley (1969-72) and Director, Institute for Desegregation Problems, School of Education, UC Berkeley (1970-72). Among his publications are *Politics of Southern Equality: Law & Social Change in a Mississippi County* (1970), with co-author, *The Political Web of American Schools* (1972), *The Polity in the School: Political Perspectives on Education* (1975). He serves as education co-editor for *Policy Studies Journal.*